Revolution and Romanticism, 1789-1834
A series of facsimile reprints chosen and introduced by
Jonathan Wordsworth
University Lecturer in Romantic Studies at Oxford

Baillie
Poems 1790

Joanna Baillie
Poems
1790

Woodstock Books
Oxford and New York
1994

This edition first published 1994 by
Woodstock Books
Spelsbury House, Spelsbury, Oxford OX7 3JR
and
Woodstock Books
387 Park Avenue South
New York, NY 10016-8810

ISBN 1 85477 175 2
Reproduced from a copy in the
British Library, shelf-mark 160 84885
by permission of the British Library Board
New matter copyright © Woodstock Books 1994

British Library Cataloguing in Publication Data
A catalogue record for this book is
available from the British Library

Library of Congress Cataloging-in-Publication Data
Baillie, Joanna, 1762-1851.
    Poems, 1790 / Joanna Baillie.
        p. cm. – (Revolution and romanticism, 1789-1834)
    Facsim. rept. Originally published: London: J. Johnson,
    1790.
    Reproduced from a copy in the British Library.
    ISBN 1-85477-175-2: $48.00
I. Title. II. Series.
PR4056.P64   1994
821'.7—dc20   94-22012
                                                      CIP

Printed and bound in Great Britain by
Smith Settle
Otley, West Yorkshire LS21 3JP

Introduction

Among the many volumes of the period amiably titled *Poems on various subjects*, *Poems on several occasions*, Joanna Baillie's 1790 collection has a curmudgeonly air: POEMS; *wherein it is attempted to describe* CERTAIN VIEWS OF NATURE *and of* RUSTIC MANNERS; *and also, to point out, in some instances, the different influence which the same circumstances produce on different characters*. All these instructions on one octavo titlepage. We are being buttonholed – told how to read and what to look for – by an author who doesn't even put her name to the book. It was to be the same with Baillie's second publication eight years later: A SERIES OF PLAYS: *in which it is attempted to delineate* THE STRONGER PASSIONS OF THE MIND, *each passion being the subject of* A TRAGEDY AND A COMEDY.

In both cases we are dealing with poetry written to support a theory. *A series of plays* makes clear the (still anonymous) author's intentions in a 72-page Introductory Discourse. In 1790, though her ways of thinking seem largely established, Baillie has yet to become a dramatist, and yet to formulate her views in detail. After the titlepage instructions we are permitted to start straight in:

> The cock, warm roosting 'midst his feather'd dames,
> Now lifts his beak and snuffs the morning air,
> Stretches his neck and claps his heavy wings,
> Gives three short crows, and glad his task is done,
> Low, chuckling, turns himself upon the roost,
> Then nestles down again amongst his mates.
> The lab'ring hind, who on his bed of straw,
> Beneath his home-made coverings, coarse, but warm,
> Lock'd in the kindly arms of her who spun them,
> Dreams of the gain that next year's crop should bring ...
> Now wakes from sleep at the unwelcome call,
> And finds himself but just the same poor man
> As when he went to rest ...
> He rubs his eyes, and stretches out his arms;
> Heigh ho! heigh ho! he drawls with gaping mouth,
> Then most unwillingly creeps out of bed,

And without looking-glass puts on his clothes.

(pp. 1-2)

The writer it seems has a sense of humour. The first
'character' introduced after the weighty claims of her
titlepage is a cock. Responding to the 'circumstance' of
morning, he crows perfunctorily, and nestles back amongst
his mates. No less comfortable with his single wife, the
human labourer stretches, yawns, and creeps unwillingly
into the day. There can be no doubt that we have witnessed a
scene of 'rustic manners', and one in which the same
circumstance has produced on different characters a
different influence. At the same time, Baillie's poetry has
offered a charming and unusual mixture of observation and
improbability. No cock before or since has 'snuffed' the air,
or crowed to rule, yet the arms of the labourer's wife, and the
coarse blankets she has woven, touch us with their tender
actuality.

Baillie takes her theorizing seriously, but fortunately does
not push it at us all the time. Half way through the 1790
volume she offers a series of four lovers, with four different
temperaments (melancholy, cheerful, proud, and sound-
hearted), each of whom says farewell to his mistress
(variously Phillis and Phill.) in three-and-a-half not very
inspiring pages. Later she presents 'Addresses to the Night'
from, a fearful mind, a discontented mind, a sorrowful mind,
and a joyful mind. It is all a bit mechanical, and doesn't bring
out her best poetry. As playwright Baillie will claim that her
drama is based on dominant passions – love in *Count Basil*
and *The tryal*, hate in *De Monfort* – but the plays work, when
they work at all, despite the theory. Consuming passion cuts
against character and idiosyncracy; it is difficult to show in
its beginnings, and once established tends to be
monotonous. The 1790 studies are an attempt to portray
mood, without personality – temperament, with no
narrative implication. They have the potential to become
dramatic monologues, but the voices are thin. Sameness of
style masks intended difference of attitude. Even when the
writing itself is good, it is not easy to tell the moods apart.

Despite the violence of the third line, and the langour of the fourth, the cloud-study of *Address to the night* (4) –

> Athwart the sky in scatter'd bands they range
> From shape to shape, transform'd in endless change;
> Then piece-meal torn, in ragged portions stray,
> Or thinly spreading, slowly melt away. (p.137)

– is the product, allegedly, of a joyful mind.

It is the underlying assumptions that give interest to Baillie's attempts to portray mood and temperament. 'Into whatever scenes the novelist may conduct us', she writes in the Introductory Discourse of 1798,

still is our attention most sensibly awake to every touch faithful to nature; still are we upon the watch for every thing that speaks to us of ourselves.

The fair field of what is properly called poetry, is enriched with so many beauties, that in it we are often tempted to forget what we really are, and what kind of beings we belong to. Who, in the enchanted regions of simile, metaphor, allegory and description, can remember the plain order of things in this every-day world? From heroes whose majestick forms rise like a lofty tower, whose eyes are lightening, whose arms are irresistible, whose course is like the storms of heaven, bold and exalted sentiments we will readily receive ... I will venture, however, to say, that amidst all this decoration and ornament, all this loftiness and refinement, let one simple trait of the human heart, one expression of passion genuine and true to nature, be introduced, and it will stand forth alone in the boldness of reality, whilst the false and unnatural around it, fades away on every side, like the rising exhalations of the morning. (*Series of plays*, 20-1)

In an impeccably natural image, the mists of artificiality are purged, burnt off, by the presence of the genuine. It is clear that Baillie's thinking in the Introductory Address was known to Coleridge and Wordsworth as they worked on *Lyrical ballads*, and influenced the wording of the Advertisement. By this date, however, there was a trend towards naturalness and simplicity that had been less obvious in 1790.

Baillie of course was Scottish. She and her mother and sister moved to London in 1784, but she had been educated in Glasgow, where her father was for a time Professor of Divinity. She would have known Blair's primitivist *Dissertation on Ossian* (1765) and *Lectures on rhetoric and belles lettres* (1783). And she knew Burns (Kilmarnock 1786, London 1787), who made the link between ancient poetry of the heart – spurious in the case of Ossian – and its modern rural equivalent. Where both Susannah Blamire (*Stoklewath*, c. 1772) and Wordsworth (*Evening walk*, 1793) base their poems of the countryside on Goldsmith's elegant *Deserted village*, Baillie's *Winter day* and its companion-piece have the uncondescending ordinariness of the *Cotter's Saturday night*:

> The toil-worn Cotter frae his labor goes –
>   This night his weekly moil is at an end –   {drudgery
> Collects his spades, his mattocks, and his hoes,
>   Hoping the morn in ease and rest to spend,
> And weary, o'er the moor, his course does hameward bend.
>
> At length his lonely Cot appears in view,
>   Beneath the shelter of an aged tree;
> Th'expectant wee-things, toddlan, stacher through   [stagger
>   To meet their Dad, wi' flichterin' noise and glee.
> His wee bit ingle, blinkan bonilie,   [little fire
>   His clean hearth-stane, his thrifty wifie's smile,
> The lisping infant, prattling on his knee,
>   Does a' his weary kiaugh and care beguile,   [anxiety
> And makes him quite forget his labor and his toil.
>   (Kilmarnock, 125-6)

Burns is not at his best, but the idiom he creates, for an English public and with English sources in mind, could be assimilated without the pastiche implied in copying the broader Scottish poems. Writing a free blank verse, willing to use both the shortened line and the extra syllable, Baillie creates a poetry that moves more easily than Burns's spenserians, and has the same power of tender observation:

> On goes the seething pot with morning cheer,
> For which some little wishful hearts await,
> Who, peeping from the bed-clothes, spy, well pleas'd,
> The cheery light that blazes on the wall,
> And bawl for leave to rise. –
> Their busy mother knows not where to turn,

Her morning work comes now so thick upon her.
One she must help to tye his little coat,
Unpin his cap, and seek another's shoe.
When all is o'er, out to the door they run,
With new comb'd sleeky hair, and glist'ning cheeks,
Each with some little project in his head.
One on the ice must try his new sol'd shoes:
To view his well-set trap another hies,
In hopes to find some poor unwary bird
(No worthless prize) entangled in his snare;
Whilst one, less active, with round rosy face,
Spreads out his purple fingers to the fire,
And peeps, most wishfully, into the pot. (pp. 3-4)

Looking back, Baillie recalled just one review of *Poems*
1790. It was a significant one, however, written by the
Reverend William Enfield, later to publish an essay (*Is verse
essential to poetry?*) that played its part in the genealogy of
Lyrical ballads. In the *Monthly review* for November 1791,
Enfield recommended Baillie's poetry: to 'those readers
whose taste is not too refined, or too fastidious, to be pleased
with true and lively pictures of nature, sketched with a
careless hand' – readers, 'who are capable of discerning and
admiring the fair form of simplicity, though negligently clad
in a rustic garb'. He is anxious, but he is judicious too. In
important ways the anonymous publication in front of him
was unusual. The poems

can, individually, boast no wild fictions to seize the fancy; and they
have little of that richness of melody which, in many of our modern
poets, so sweetly captivates the ear: but they contain minute and
circumstantial descriptions of natural objects, scenes, and characters;
and they express, in easy though peculiar language, the feelings of
undisguised and uncorrupted nature.

On every point Enfield is right. Neither here, nor in the
plays, does Baillie have 'wild fictions' to seize the
imagination. Even in her fluent stanzaic poems, she is far
from being one of the 'sweet singers' of the '80s, captivating
the ear with melody. With its admixture of Scottish ('red and
grumly', 'black and grumly'), her language is truly 'easy
though peculiar'. Above all, at this turning-point in

literature, she does indeed show the 'feelings of undisguised and uncorrupted nature'. There is no artifice about the child who 'Spreads out his purple fingers to the fire, / And peeps, most wishfully, into the pot'. Burns would have been proud to own him – and Wordsworth too.

Baillie has a voice of her own, and it is genuinely new. She should be valued in her own right, not for what may seem anticipations of later, greater verse. But no reader of the *Ruined cottage* could fail, as they come upon the *Lamentation*, to think of Margaret, linked in death to the image of the 'rank speargrass', 'By mist and silent raindrops silvered o'er':

> The fallen leaves light rustling o'er thee pass,
> And o'er thee waves the rank and dewy grass (p. 68)

And no reader of the *Prelude* could fail to hear in Baillie's poem the vocabulary and associative thinking of Wordsworth's 'spot of time' ('when storm / And rain beat on my roof at midnight … The workings of my spirit thence are brought'):

> At ev'ry wailing of the midnight wind
> Thy lowly dwelling comes into my mind.
> When rain beats on my roof, wild storms abroad,
> I think upon thy bare and beaten sod … (pp. 69-70)

That Wordsworth did borrow from Baillie, we know. Two to three months before the *Prelude* 'spots of time' were composed, he had based *There was a boy* on a speech in *De Monfort*. Could he perhaps in 1798-9 have had access to *Poems* 1790 as well as the *Series of plays?* It is a curious thought that if he did, he might well not have known that the volumes were by the same writer. Baillie's anonymity was carefully preserved.

Among the pairings characteristic of Baillie's *Poems* (and of her way of thinking) is the *Story of other times, somewhat in imitation of the poems of Ossian* and the *Storm-beat maid, somewhat after the style of our old English ballads*. Blair had described MacPherson's 'translation' of the Celtic poet, Ossian, as having 'The two great characteristics of … tenderness and sublimity':

His poetry, more perhaps than that of any other writer, deserves to be styled, *The Poetry of the heart*. It is a heart penetrated with noble sentiments, and with sublime and tender passions; a heart that glows, and kindles the fancy; a heart that is full, and pours itself forth.

(Works of Ossian, 2 vols 1765, ii 384-5)

By 1790 most readers accepted that *Fingal* (1762) and *Temora* (1763) were fakes. But Ossian had a special appeal. Those wishing for the genuine, the pure, the primitive (Goethe among them) were provided by Macpherson with a sort of meaningful plangency, half-told stories endlessly evocative of lives and passions purer than their own. Baillie catches the tones, without (any more than anyone else) being able to move the poetry on beyond romantic nostalgia:

> Matchless in the days of their love were Lochallen and the
> daughter of Lorma.
> But their beauty has ceas'd on Arthula; and the place of
> their rest is unknown.   (p.151)

Ballads were a different matter. Not only was the past they belonged to genuine, the form allowed for innovation. Baillie's *Storm-beat maid* is an important poem:

> All shrouded in the winter snow,
>   The maiden held her way;
> Nor chilly winds that roughly blow,
>   Nor dark night could her stay.
>
> O'er hill and dale, through bush and briar,
>   She on her journey kept ... (p. 97)

Sad, beautiful, living in an other-worldly realm of the mind that is all her own, the Storm-beat Maid travels through a winter landscape of which she takes no heed. Though ghostly, she is alive. Her presence, though, is such that it can best be described in terms of the natural world:

> Her face is like an early morn,
>   Dimm'd with the nightly dew;
> Her skin is like the sheeted torn,   [*Read* thorn? Like a thorn-
>   Her eyes are wat'ry blue.   bush, 'sheeted' with blossom]
>
> And tall and slender is her form,

Like willow o'er the brook;
But on her brow there broods a storm,
    And restless is her look. (pp. 102-3)

Travelling on, insensible of all around her, the Maid comes
to a castle where a wedding-feast is taking place. As we
suspect, it is her lover who is to be married; what we do not
expect is his reaction to her coming:

    cursed be the woman's art,
  That lur'd me to her snare!
And cursed be the faithless heart
  That left thee to despair!

Yet now I'll hold thee to my side,
  Tho' worthless I have been,
Nor friends, nor wealth, nor dizen'd bride,   [bedecked
  Shall ever stand between.

When thou art weary and depress'd,
  I'll lull thee to thy sleep;
And when dark fancies vex thy breast,
  I'll sit by thee and weep.

I'll tend thee like a restless child
  Where'er thy rovings be;
Nor gesture keen, nor eye-ball wild,
  Shall turn my love from thee.

Baillie has written in 1790 what is by any standards a lyrical
ballad. The flimsy plot has no significance; everything in the
Storm-beat maid depends on states of mind. In terms of
Wordsworth's 1800 Preface, 'the feeling therein developed
gives importance to the action and situation, and not the
action and situation to the feeling'.

  In fact it might seem that Baillie has not merely invented
the Wordsworthian lyrical ballad, she has combined in one
poem its two major different aspects. The lover's response in
the final lines anticipates the Alfoxden poetry of relationship
and tenderness (see also *Mother to her waking infant*, pp. 170-
3), and with it the interest in abnormal states of mind. Baillie,
however, is writing in the ballad-metre used in four out of
five of the Goslar Lucy Poems. The metre is a common one
(occurring, for instance, in the *Ancient mariner* and *We are*

seven), but the coincidence of rhythm heightens our sense that the Storm-beat Maid and Lucy belong to the same uncanny world of imagination. The Maid, of course, is mad; but her madness is never exemplified in act or speech. It is felt as a powerful strangeness. To use the terms that Wordsworth applied to Lucy, her character is 'spiritualized'.

With the *Lamentation* it looks as though resemblances of mood and situation may have brought Baillie's phrasing to mind as Wordsworth worked on the *Ruined cottage* and *Prelude* 'spots of time'. With the *Storm-beat maid* it is easy to imagine his being impressed by the poem, and at some later stage writing *Lucy Gray* (first of the Lucy Poems, and nearest to ballad narrative) in the same metre and something of the same idiom. In the case of *Address to the muses* we see Baillie at her cheekiest, and Wordsworth at his closest to direct borrowing. 'I to the muses have been bound', he writes, as the final scene of the *Idiot boy* is about to begin,

> These fourteen years, by strong indentures;
> Oh gentle muses! let me tell
> But half of what to him befel,
> For sure he met with strange adventures.
>
> Oh gentle muses, is this kind?
> Why will ye thus my suit repel?
> Why of your further aid bereave me?
> (*Lyrical ballads*, 172)

Using the same tones exactly, and the same repetition, Baillie had written in consecutive stanzas of *Address to the muses*,

> O lovely sisters! is it true,
> That they are all inspired by you? …
>
> O lovely sisters! well it shews
> How wide and far your bounty flows:
> Then why from me withhold your beams? (pp. 76-7)

Engaged two weeks later on *Peter Bell*, Wordsworth invokes, not the muses, but 'spirits of the mind', wonderful half-comic presences who similarly do, and do not, represent the human imagination:

Your presence I have often felt
In darkness and the stormy night;
And well I know, if need there be,
Ye can put forth your agency
When earth is calm, and heaven is bright.

Then, coming from the wayward world,
That powerful world in which ye dwell,
Come, Spirits of the Mind! and try,
Tonight, beneath the moonlight sky,
What may be done with Peter Bell! (*Peter Bell*, 59)

Baillie in *Address to the muses* had written:

Ye are the spirits who preside
In earth, and air, and ocean wide;
In hissing flood, and crackling fire;
In horror dread, and tumult dire;
In stilly calm, and stormy wind,
And rule the answ'ring changes in the human mind.

High on the tempest-beaten hill,
Your misty shapes ye shift at will;
The wild fantastic clouds ye form;
Your voice is in the midnight storm … (p. 78)

Baillie, like the Wordsworth of *Lyrical ballads*, is funny, sad, tender, affectionate, capable of many moods of 'passion genuine and true to nature'. As a playwright she achieved a very high reputation among her contemporaries. Looking back, though, it seems a pity that such a good writer should have turned to drama in a period when no one quite pulled it off. She had it in her to be a poet of real stature.

J. W.

P O E M S, &c.

P O E M S;

WHEREIN IT IS ATTEMPTED TO DESCRIBE

CERTAIN VIEWS OF NATURE

AND OF

RUSTIC MANNERS;

A N D   A L S O,

TO POINT OUT, IN SOME INSTANCES, THE
DIFFERENT INFLUENCE WHICH THE SAME
CIRCUMSTANCES PRODUCE ON DIFFERENT
CHARACTERS.

L O N D O N:

PRINTED FOR J. JOHNSON, SAINT PAUL'S CHURCH-YARD.

MDCCXC.

A WINTER DAY.

THE cock, warm roosting 'midst his feather'd dames,
Now lifts his beak and snuffs the morning air,
Stretches his neck and claps his heavy wings,
Gives three hoarse crows, and glad his task is done;
Low, chuckling, turns himself upon the roost,
Then nestles down again amongst his mates.
The lab'ring hind, who on his bed of straw,
Beneath his home-made coverings, coarse, but warm,
Lock'd in the kindly arms of her who spun them,
Dreams of the gain that next year's crop should bring;
Or at some fair disposing of his wool,
Or by some lucky and unlook'd-for bargain,
Fills his skin purse with heaps of tempting gold,
Now wakes from sleep at the unwelcome call,

And finds himself but juft the fame poor man

As when he went to reft.——

He hears the blaft againft his window beat,

And wifhes to himfelf he were a lord,

That he might lie a-bed.——

He rubs his eyes, and ftretches out his arms;

Heigh ho! heigh ho! he drawls with gaping mouth,

Then moft unwillingly creeps out of bed,

And without looking-glafs puts on his clothes.

With rueful face he blows the fmother'd fire,

And lights his candle at the red'ning coal;

Firft fees that all be right amongft his cattle,

Then hies him to the barn with heavy tread,

Printing his footfteps on the new fall'n fnow.

From out the heap of corn he pulls his fheaves,

Diflodging the poor red-breaft from his fhelter,

Where all the live-long night he flept fecure;

But now afrighted, with uncertain flight

He flutters round the walls, to feek fome hole,

At which he may efcape out to the froft.

And

And now the flail, high whirling o'er his head,

Defcends with force upon the jumping fheave,

Whilft every rugged wall, and neighb'ring cot

Re-echoes back the noife of his ftrokes.

   The fam'ly cares call next upon the wife

To quit her mean but comfortable bed.

And firft fhe ftirs the fire, and blows the flame,

Then from her heap of fticks, for winter ftor'd,

An armful brings; loud crackling as they burn,

Thick fly the red fparks upward to the roof,

While flowly mounts the fmoke in wreathy clouds.

On goes the feething pot with morning cheer,

For which fome little wifhful hearts await,

Who, peeping from the bed-clothes, fpy, well pleas'd,

The cheery light that blazes on the wall,

And bawl for leave to rife.————

Their bufy mother knows not where to turn,

Her morning work comes now fo thick upon her.

One fhe muft help to tye his little coat,

Unpin

Unpin his cap, and seek another's shoe.

When all is o'er, out to the door they run,

With new comb'd sleeky hair, and glist'ning cheeks,

Each with some little project in his head.

One on the ice must try his new sol'd shoes:

To view his well-set trap another hies,

In hopes to find some poor unwary bird

(No worthless prize) entangled in his snare;

Whilst one, less active, with round rosy face,

Spreads out his purple fingers to the fire,

And peeps, most wishfully, into the pot.

But let us leave the warm and cheerful house,

To view the bleak and dreary scene without,

And mark the dawning of a winter day.

For now the morning vapour, red and grumly,

Rests heavy on the hills; and o'er the heav'ns

Wide spreading forth in lighter gradual shades,

Just faintly colours the pale muddy sky.

Then slowly from behind the southern hills,

Inlarg'd

Inlarg'd and ruddy looks the rifing fun,

Shooting his beams afkance the hoary wafte,

Which gild the brow of ev'ry fwelling height,

And deepen every valley with a fhade.

The crufted window of each fcatter'd cot,

The icicles that fringe the thatched roof,

The new fwept flide upon the frozen pool,

All lightly glance, new kindled with his rays;

And e'en the rugged face of fcowling Winter

Looks fomewhat gay. But for a little while

He lifts his glory o'er the bright'ning earth,

Then hides his head behind a mifty cloud.

The birds now quit their holes and lurking fheds,

Moft mute and melancholy, where thro' night

All neftling clofe to keep each other warm,

In downy fleep they had forgot their hardfhips ;

But not to chant and carol in the air,

Or lightly fwing upon fome waving bough,

And merrily return each other's notes ;

B 3   No,

No ; filently they hop from bufh to bufh,

Yet find no feeds to ftop their craving want,

Then bend their flight to the low fmoking cot,

Chirp on the roof, or at the window peck,

To tell their wants to thofe who lodge within.

The poor lank hare flies homeward to his den,

But little burthen'd with his nightly meal

Of wither'd greens grubb'd from the farmer's garden ;

A poor and fcanty portion fnatch'd in fear ;

And fearful creatures, forc'd abroad by want,

Are now to ev'ry enemy a prey.

The hufbandman lays bye his heavy flail,

And to the houfe returns, where on him wait

His fmoking breakfaft and impatient children ;

Who, fpoon in hand, and longing to begin,

Towards the door caft many a weary look

To fee their dad come in.———

Then round they fit, a chearful company,

All eagerly begin, and with heap'd fpoons

Befmear

Befmear from ear to ear their rofy cheeks.

The faithful dog ftands by his mafter's fide

Wagging his tail, and looking in his face;

While humble pufs pays court to all around,

And purs and rubs them with her furry fides;

Nor goes this little flattery unrewarded.

But the laborious fit not long at table;

The grateful father lifts his eyes to heav'n

To blefs his God, whofe ever bounteous hand

Him and his little ones doth daily feed;

Then rifes fatisfied to work again.

The chearful roufing noife of induftry

Is heard, with varied founds, thro' all the village.

The humming wheel, the thrifty houfewife's tongue,

Who fcolds to keep her maidens at their work,

Rough grating cards, and voice of fqualing children

Iffue from every houfe.———

But, hark!—the fportfman from the neighb'ring hedge

His thunder fends!—loud bark each village cur;

Up

Up from her wheel each curious maiden ftarts,

And haftens to the door, whilft matrons chide,

Yet run to look themfelves, in fpite of thrift,

And all the little town is in a ftir.

Strutting before, the cock leads forth his train,

And, chuckling near the barn among the ftraw,

Reminds the farmer of his morning's fervice;

His grateful mafter throws a lib'ral handful;

They flock about it, whilft the hungry fparrows

Perch'd on the roof, look down with envious eye,

Then, aiming well, amidft the feeders light,

And feize upon the feaft with greedy bill,

Till angry partlets peck them off the field.

But at a diftance, on the leaflefs tree,

All woe be gone, the lonely blackbird fits;

The cold north wind ruffles his gloffy feathers;

Full oft' he looks, but dare not make approach;

Then turns his yellow bill to peck his fide,

And claps his wings clofe to his fharpen'd breaft.

The

The wand'ring fowler, from behind the hedge,
Faftens his eye upon him, points his gun,
And firing wantonly as at a mark,
E'en lays him low in that fame cheerful fpot
Which oft' hath echo'd with his ev'ning's fong.

    The day now at its height, the pent-up kine
Are driven from their ftalls to take the air.
How ftupidly they ftare! and feel how ftrange!
They open wide their fmoking mouths to low,
But fcarcely can their feeble found be heard;
Then turn and lick themfelves, and ftep by ftep
Move dull and heavy to their ftalls again.
In fcatter'd groups the little idle boys
With purple fingers, moulding in the fnow
Their icy ammunition, pant for war;
And, drawing up in oppofite array,
Send forth a mighty fhower of well aim'd balls,
Whilft little hero's try their growing ftrength,
And burn to beat the en'my off the field.

                      Or

Or on the well worn ice in eager throngs,

Aiming their race, fhoot rapidly along,

Trip up each other's heels, and on the furface

With knotted fhoes, draw many a chalky line.

Untir'd of play, they never ceafe their fport

Till the faint fun has almoft run his courfe,

And threat'ning clouds, flow rifing from the north,

Spread grumly darknefs o'er the face of heav'n;

Then, by degrees, they fcatter to their homes,

With many a broken head and bloody nofe,

To claim their mothers' pity, who, moft fkilful,

Cures all their troubles with a bit of bread.

The night comes on a pace——

Chill blows the blaft, and drives the fnow in wreaths.

Now ev'ry creature looks around for fhelter,

And, whether man or beaft, all move alike

Towards their feveral homes; and happy they

Who have a houfe to fcreen them from the cold!

Lo, o'er the froft a rev'rend form advances!

His

His hair white as the fnow on which he treads,

His forehead mark'd with many a care-worn furrow,

Whofe feeble body, bending o'er a ftaff,

Still fhew that once it was the feat of ftrength,

Tho' now it fhakes like fome old ruin'd tow'r.

Cloth'd indeed, but not difgrac'd with rags,

He ftill maintains that decent dignity

Which well becomes thofe who have ferv'd their country.

With tott'ring fteps he to the cottage moves :

The wife within, who hears his hollow cough,

And patt'ring of his ftick upon the threfhold,

Sends out her little boy to fee who's there.

The child looks up to view the ftranger's face,

And feeing it enlighten'd with a fmile,

Holds out his little hand to lead him in.

Rous'd from her work, the mother turns her head,

And fees them, not ill-pleas'd.———

The ftranger whines not with a piteous tale,

But only afks a little, to relieve

A poor old foldier's wants.———

The

The gentle matron brings the ready chair,
And bids him fit, to reft his wearied limbs,
And warm himfelf before her blazing fire.
The children, full of curiofity,
Flock round, and with their fingers in their mouths,
Stand ftaring at him; whilft the ftranger, pleas'd,
Takes up the youngeft boy upon his knee,
Proud of its feat, it wags its little feet,
And prates, and laughs, and plays with his white locks.
But foon the foldier's face lays off its fmiles ;
His thoughtful mind is turn'd on other days,
When his own boys were wont to play around him,
Who now lie diftant from their native land
In honourable, but untimely graves.
He feels how helplefs and forlorn he is,
And bitter tears gufh from his dim-worn eyes.
His toilfome daily labour at an end,
In comes the wearied mafter of the houfe,
And marks with fatisfaction his old gueft,
With all his children round.——

His

His honeſt heart is fill'd with manly kindneſs;

He bids him ſtay, and ſhare their homely meal,

And take with them his quarters for the night.

The weary wanderer thankfully accepts,

And, ſeated with the cheerful family,

Around the plain but hoſpitable board,

Forgets the many hardſhips he has paſs'd.

When all are ſatisfied, about the fire

They draw their ſeats, and form a cheerful ring.

The thrifty houſewife turns her ſpinning wheel;

The huſband, uſeful even in his reſt,

A little baſket weaves of willow twigs,

To bear her eggs to town on market days;

And work but ſerves t'enliven converſation.

Some idle neighbours now come ſtraggling in,

Draw round their chairs, and widen out the circle.

Without a glaſs the tale and jeſt go round;

And every one, in his own native way,

Does what he can to cheer the merry group.

Each

Each tells fome little ftory of himfelf,

That conftant fubject upon which mankind,

Whether in court or country, love to dwell.

How at a fair he fav'd a fimple clown

From being trick'd in buying of a cow;

Or laid a bet upon his horfe's head

Againft his neighbour's, bought for twice his price,

Which fail'd not to repay his better fkill:

Or on a harveft day, bound in an hour

More fheaves of corn than any of his fellows,

Tho' ne'er fo keen, could do in twice the time.

But chief the landlord, at his own fire-fide,

Doth claim the right of being liften'd to;

Nor dares a little bawling tongue be heard,

Tho' but in play, to break upon his ftory.

The children fit and liften with the reft;

And fhould the youngeft raife its little voice,

The careful mother, ever on the watch,

And always pleas'd with what her hufband fays,

Gives it a gentle tap upon the fingers,

Or

Or ſtops its ill tim'd prattle with a kiſs.

The ſoldier next, but not unaſk'd, begins,

And tells in better ſpeech what he has ſeen;

Making his ſimple audience to ſhrink

With tales of war and blood. They gaze upon him,

And almoſt weep to ſee the man ſo poor,

So bent and feeble, helpleſs and forlorn,

That oft' has ſtood undaunted in the battle

Whilſt thund'ring cannons ſhook the quaking earth,

And ſhowering bullets hiſs'd around his head.

With little care they paſs away the night,

Till time draws on when they ſhould go to bed;

Then all break up, and each retires to reſt

With peaceful mind, nor torn with vexing cares,

Nor dancing with the unequal beat of pleaſure.

But long accuſtom'd to obſerve the weather,

The labourer cannot lay him down in peace

Till he has look'd to mark what bodes the night.

He turns the heavy door, thruſts out his head,

Seⱥ

Sees wreathes of ſnow heap'd up on ev'ry ſide,

And black and grumly all above his head,

Save when a red gleam ſhoots along the waſte

To make the gloomy night more terrible.

Loud blows the northern blaſt——

He hears it hollow grumbling from afar,

Then, gath'rıng ſtrength, roll on with doubl'd might,

And break in dreadful bellowings o'er his head;

Like pithleſs ſaplings bend the vexed trees,

And their wide branches crack. He ſhuts the door,

And, thankful for the roof that covers him,

Hies him to bed.

A SUMMER

A SUMMER DAY.

THE dark-blue clouds of night in dusky lines,
Drawn wide and streaky o'er the purer sky,
Wear faint the morning purple on their skirts.
The stars that full and bright shone in the west,
But dimly twinkle to the stedfast eye;
And seen, and vanishing, and seen again,
Like dying tapers smoth'ring in their sockets,
Appear at last shut from the face of heav'n;
Whilst every lesser flame which shone by night,
The flashy meteor from the op'ning cloud,
That shoots full oft' acrofs the dusky sky;
Or wand'ring fire which looks acrofs the marsh,
Beaming like candle in a lonely cot,

To

To cheer the hopes of the benighted trav'ller,

Till fwifter than the very change of thought,

It fhifts from place to place, efcapes his glance,

And makes him wond'ring rub his doubtful eyes;

Or humble glow-worm, or the filver moth,

Which caft a feeble glimm'ring o'er the green,

All die away.——

For now the fun, flow moving in his grandeur,

Above the eaftern mountains lifts his head.

The webs of dew fpread o'er the hoary lawn,

The fmooth clear bofom of the fettled pool,

The polifh'd ploughfhare on the diftant field,

Catch fire from him, and dart their new got beams

Upon the dazzled eye.

The new-wak'd birds upon the branches hop,

Peck their foft down, and briftle out their feathers;

Then ftretch their throats and tune their morning fong;

Whilft ftately crows, high fwinging o'er their heads,

Upon the topmoft boughs, in lordly pride,

Mix

Mix their hoarſe croaking with the linnet's note;

Till gather'd cloſer in a ſable band,

They take their flight to ſeek their daily food.

The village labourer, with careful mind,

As ſoon as doth the morning light appear,

Opens his eyes with the firſt darting ray

That pierces thro' the window of his cot,

And quits his eaſy bed; then o'er the field,

With lengthen'd ſwinging ſtrides, betakes his way,

Bearing his ſpade and hoe acroſs his ſhoulder,

Seen from afar clear glancing in the ſun,

And with good will begins his daily work.

The ſturdy ſun-burnt boy drives forth the cattle,

And vain of power, bawls to the lagging kine,

Who fain would ſtay to crop the tender ſhoots

Of the green tempting hedges as they paſs;

Or beats the gliſt'ning buſhes with his club,

To pleaſe his fancy with a ſhower of dew,

And frighten the poor birds who lurk within.

At ev'ry open door, thro' all the village,

Half

Half naked children, half awake, are feen
Scratching their heads, and blinking to the light;
Till roufed by degrees, they run about,
Or rolling in the fun, amongft the fand
Build many a little houfe, with heedful art.
The houfewife tends within, her morning care;
And ftooping 'midft her tubs of curdled milk,
With bufy patience, draws the clear green whey
From the prefs'd fides of the pure fnowy curd;
Whilft her brown dimpled maid, with tuck'd-up fleeve,
And fwelling arm, affifts her in her toil.
Pots fmoke, pails rattle, and the warm confufion
Still thickens on them, till within its mould,
With careful hands, they prefs the well-wrought curd.

So goes the morning, till the pow'rful fun
High in the heav'ns fends forth his ftrengthen'd beams,
And all the frefhnefs of the morn is fled.
The fweating trav'ller throws his burden down,
And leans his weary fhoulder 'gainft a tree.

The

The idle horfe upon the graffy field

Rolls on his back, nor heeds the tempting clover.

The fwain leaves off his labour, and returns

Slow to his houfe with heavy fober fteps,

Where on the board his ready breakfaft plac'd,

Invites the eye, and his right cheerful wife

Doth kindly ferve him with unfeign'd good will.

No fparkling dew-drops hang upon the grafs;

Forth fteps the mower with his glitt'ring fcythe,

In fnowy fhirt, and doublet all untrac'd,

White moves he o'er the ridge, with fideling bend,

And lays the waving grafs in many a heap.

In ev'ry field, in ev'ry fwampy mead,

The cheerful voice of induftry is heard;

The hay-cock rifes, and the frequent rake

Sweeps on the yellow hay, in heavy wreaths,

Leaving the fmooth green meadow bare behind.

The old and young, the weak and ftrong are there,

And, as they can, help on the cheerful work.

The father jeers his awkward half-grown lad,

C 3

Who trails his tawdry armful o'er the field,

Nor does he fear the jeering to repay.

The village oracle, and fimple maid,

Jeft in their turns, and raife the ready laugh;

For there authority, hard favour'd, frowns not;

All are companions in the gen'ral glee,

And cheerful complaifance ftill thro' their roughnefs,

With placid look enlightens ev'ry face.

Some more advanced raife the tow'ring rick,

Whilft on its top doth ftand the parifh toaft

In loofe attire, and fwelling ruddy cheek;

With taunts and harmlefs mock'ry fhe receives

The tofs'd-up heaps from the brown gaping youth,

Who ftaring at her, takes his aim awry,

Whilft half the load comes tumbling on himfelf.

Loud is her laugh, her voice is heard afar;

Each mower, bufied in the diftant field,

The carter, trudging on his diftant way,

The fhrill found know, caft up their hats in air,

And roar acrofs the fields to catch her notice:

She

She waves her arm, and ſhakes her head at them,

And then renews her work with double ſpirit.

Thus do they jeſt, and laugh away their toil,

Till the bright ſun, full in his middle courſe,

Shoots down his fierceſt beams, which none may brave.

The ſtouteſt arm hangs liſtleſs by its ſide,

And the broad ſhoulder'd youth begins to fail.

But to the weary, lo ! there comes relief !

A troop of welcome children, o'er the lawn,

With ſlow and wary ſteps, their burthens bring.

Some bear upon their heads large baſkets, heap'd

With piles of barley bread, and guſty cheeſe,

And ſome full pots of milk and cooling whey.

Beneath the branches of a ſpreading tree,

Or by the ſhad'wy ſide of the tall rick,

They ſpread their homely fare, and ſeated round,

Taſte all the pleaſure that a feaſt can give.

A drowzy indolence now hangs on all,

And ev'ry creature ſeeks ſome place of reſt,

Screen'd

Screen'd from the violence of the oppreſſive heat.

No ſcatter'd flocks are ſeen upon the lawn,

Nor chirping birds among the buſhes heard.

Within the narrow ſhadow of the cot

The ſleepy dog lies ſtretched on his ſide,

Nor heeds the heavy-footed paſſenger ;

At noiſe of feet but half his eye-lid lifts,

Then gives a feeble growl, and ſleeps again :

Whilſt puſs, leſs nice, e'en in the ſcorching window,

On t'other ſide, ſits winking to the ſun.

No ſound is heard but humming of the bee,

For ſhe alone retires not from her labour,

Nor leaves a meadow flower unſought for gain.

Heavy and ſlow ſo paſs the mid-day hours,

Till gently bending on the ridge's top,

The heavy ſeeded graſs begins to wave,

And the high branches of the ſlender poplar

Shiver aloft in air their ruſtling leaves.

Cool breaths the riſing breeze, and with it wakes

The

The worn out ſpirit from its ſtate of ſtupor.

The lazy boy ſprings from his moſſy bed,

To chace the gaudy tempting butterfly,

Who ſpreading on the graſs its mealy wings,

Oft lights within his reach, e'en at his feet,

Yet ſtill eludes his graſp, and o'er his head

Light hov'ring round, or mounted high in air

Temps his young eye, and wearies out his limbs.

The drouzy dog, who feels the kindly breeze

That paſſing o'er him, lifts his ſhaggy ear,

Begins to ſtretch him, on his legs half-rais'd,

Till fully wak'd, with briſtling cock'd-up tail,

He makes the village echo to his bark.

But let us not forget the buſy maid

Who, by the ſide of the clear pebly ſtream,

Spreads out her ſnowy linens to the ſun,

And ſheds with lib'ral hand the chryſtal ſhow'r

O'er many a fav'rite piece of fair attire,

Revolving in her mind her gay appearance

In

In all this drefs, at fome approaching fair.

The dimpling half-check'd fmile, and mutt'ring lip

Betray the fecret workings of her fancy,

And flattering thoughts of the complacent mind.

There little vagrant bands of truant boys

Amongft the bufhes try their harmlefs tricks;

Whilft fome a fporting in the fhallow ftream

Tofs up the lafhing water round their heads,

Or ftrive with wily art to catch the trout,

Or 'twixt their fingers grafp the flipp'ry eel.

The fhepherd-boy fits finging on the bank,

To pafs away the weary lonely hours,

Weaving with art his little crown of rufhes,

A guiltlefs eafy crown that brings no care,

Which having made he places on his head,

And leaps and fkips about, and bawls full loud

To fome companion, lonely as himfelf,

Far in the diftant field; or elfe delighted

To hear the echo'd found of his own voice

Returning

Returning anfwer from the neighb'ring rock,
Holds no unpleafing converfe with himfelf.

Now weary labourers perceive, well-pleas'd,
The fhadows lengthen, and th' oppreffive day
With all its toil faft wearing to an end.
The fun, far in the weft, with fide-long beam
Plays on the yellow head of the round hay-cock,
And fields are checker'd with fantaftic fhapes
Or tree, or fhrub, or gate, or rugged ftone,
All lengthen'd out, in antic difproportion,
Upon the darken'd grafs.——
They finifh out their long and toilfome tafk.
Then, gathering up their rakes and fcatter'd coats,
With the lefs cumb'rous fragments of their feaft,
Return right gladly to their peaceful homes.

The village, lone and filent thro' the day,
Receiving from the fields its merry bands,
Sends forth its ev'ning found, confus'd but cheerful;

Whilft

Whilſt dogs and children, eager houſewives' tongues,

And true love ditties, in no plaintive ſtrain,

By ſhrill voic'd maid, at open window ſung;

The lowing of the home-returning kine,

The herd's low droning trump, and tinkling bell

Tied to the collar of his fav'rite ſheep,

Make no contemptible variety

To ears not over nice.——

With careleſs lounging gait, the ſaunt'ring youth

Upon his ſweetheart's open window leans,

And as ſhe turns about her buzzing wheel

Diverts her with his jokes and harmleſs taunts.

Cloſe by the cottage door, with placid mien,

The old man ſits upon his ſeat of turf,

His ſtaff with crooked head laid by his ſide,

Which oft the younger race in wanton ſport,

Gambolling round him, ſlyly ſteal away,

And ſtraddling o'er it, ſhew their horſemanſhip

By raiſing round the clouds of ſummer ſand,

While ſtill he ſmiles, yet chides them for the trick.

His

His filver locks upon his fhoulders fpread,

And not ungraceful is his ftoop of age.

No ftranger paffes him without regard;

And ev'ry neighbour ftops to wifh him well,

And afk him his opinion of the weather.

They fret not at the length of his difcourfe,

But liften with refpect to his remarks

Upon the various feafons he remembers;

For well he knows the many divers figns

Which do fortell high winds, or rain, or drought,

Or ought that may affect the rifing crop.

The filken clad, who courtly breeding boaft,

Their own difcourfe ftill fweeteft to their ears,

May grumble at the old man's lengthen'd ftory,

But here it is not fo.———

From ev'ry chimney mounts the curling fmoke,

Muddy and gray, of the new ev'ning fire;

On ev'ry window fmokes the fam'ly fupper,

Set out to cool by the attentive houfewife,

While

While cheerful groups at every door conven'd

Bawl crofs the narrow lane the parifh news,

And oft the burfting laugh difturbs the air.

But fee who comes to fet them all agag!

The weary-footed pedlar with his pack.

How ftiff he bends beneath his bulky load!

Cover'd with duft, flip-fhod, and out at elbows;

His greafy hat fits backward on his head;

His thin ftraight hair divided on his brow

Hangs lank on either fide his glift'ning cheeks,

And woe-begone, yet vacant is his face.

His box he opens and difplays his ware.

Full many a varied row of precious ftones

Caft forth their dazzling luftre to the light.

To the defiring maiden's wifhful eye

The ruby necklace fhews its tempting blaze:

The china buttons, ftamp'd with love device,

Attract the notice of the gaping youth;

Whilft ftreaming garters, faften'd to a pole,

Aloft in air their gaudy ftripes difplay,

And

And from afar the diftant ftragglers lure.

The children leave their play and round him flock;

E'en fober aged grand-dame quits her feat,

Where by the door fhe twines her lengthen'd threads,

Her fpindle ftops, and lays her diftaff by,

Then joins with ftep fedate the curious throng.

She praifes much the fafhions of her youth,

And fcorns each gaudy nonfenfe of the day;

Yet not ill-pleas'd the gloffy ribband views,

Uproll'd, and changing hues with ev'ry fold,

New meafur'd out to deck her daughter's head.

Now red, but languid, the laft weakly beams

Of the departing fun, acrofs the lawn

Deep gild the top of the long fweepy ridge,

And fhed a fcatter'd brightnefs, bright but cheerlefs,

Between the op'nings of the rifted hills;

Which like the farewell looks of fome dear friend,

That fpeaks him kind, yet fadden as they fmile,

But

But only ferve to deepen the low vale,

And make the fhadows of the night more gloomy.

The varied noifes of the cheerful village

By flow degrees now faintly die away,

And more diftinct each feeble found is heard

That gently fteals adown the river's bed,

Or thro' the wood comes with the ruffling breeze.

The white mift rifes from the fwampy glens,

And from the dappled fkirting of the heav'ns

Looks out the ev'ning ftar.———

The lover fkulking in the neighb'ring copfe,

(Whofe half-feen form fhewn thro' the thicken'd air,

Large and majeftic, makes the trav'ller ftart,

And fpreads the ftory of the haunted grove,)

Curfes the owl, whofe loud ill-omen'd fcream,

With ceafelefs fpite, robes from his watchful ear

The well known footfteps of his darling maid;

And fretful, chaces from his face the night-fly,

Who buzzing round his head doth often fkim,

With

With flutt'ring wing, acrofs his glowing cheek :

For all but him in deep and balmy fleep

Forget the toils of the oppreffive day ;

Shut is the door of ev'ry fcatter'd cot,

And filence dwells within.

NIGHT

NIGHT SCENES of OTHER TIMES.

A POEM, IN THREE PARTS.

PART I.

" THE wild winds bellow o'er my head,
   " And fpent eve's fading light;
" Where fhall I find fome friendly fhed
   " To fcreen me from the night?

   " Ah! round me lies a defert vaft,
    " No habitation near;
   " And dark and pathlefs is the wafte,
    " And fills the mind with fear

Thou

" Thou diftant tree, whofe lonely top

" Has bent to many a ftorm,

" No more canft thou deceive my hope,

" And take my lover's form ;

" For o'er thy head the dark cloud rolls,

" Black as thy blafted pride.

" How deep the angry tempeft growls

" Along the mountain's fide !

" Securely refts the mountain deer

" Within his hollow den,

" His flumber undifturb'd by fear,

" Far from the haunts of men.

" Beneath the fern the moorcock fleeps,

" And twifted adders lie ;

" Back to his rock the night-bird creeps,

" Nor gives his wonted cry.

D 2   " For

" For angry fpirits of the night

    " Ride in the troubled air,

" And to their dens, in wild affright,

    " The beafts of prey repair.

" But oh ! my love ! where do'ft thou reft ?

    " What fhelter covers thee ?

" O, may this cold and wint'ry blaft

    " But only beat on me !

" Some friendly dwelling may'ft thou find,

    " Where, undifturb'd with care,

" Thou fhalt not feel the chilly wind

    " That ruffles Marg'ret's hair.

" Ah, no ! for thou did'ft give thy word

    " To meet me on the way ;

" Nor friendly roof, nor coaftly board

    " Will tempt a lover's ftay.

                " O, raife

" O, raife thy voice, if thou art near !

   " Its weakeft found were blifs :

" What other found my heart can cheer

   " In fuch a gloom as this ?

" But from the hills with ftunning found

   " The dafhing torrents fall ;

" Loud is the raging tempeft round,

   " And mocks a lover's call.

" Ha ! fee acrofs the dreary wafte

   " A gentle form appears !

" It is my love, my cares are paft,

   " How vain were all my fears ?"

The form approach'd, but fad and flow,

   Nor with a lover's tread ;

And from his cheek the youthful glow,

   And greeting fmile was fled.

Dim

Dim fadnefs hung upon his brow ;

    Fix'd was his beamlefs eye :

His face was like the moon-light bow

    Upon a win'try fky.

And fix'd and ghaftly to the fight,

    His ftrengthen'd features rofe ;

And bended was his graceful height,

    And bloody were his clothes.

" O Marg'ret, calm thy troubled breaft !

    " Thy forrow now is vain :

" Thy Edward from his peaceful reft

    " Shall ne'er return again.

" A treach'rous friend has brought me low,

    " And fix'd my early doom ;

" And laid my corpfe, with feigned woe,

    " Beneath a vaulted tomb

                                                               " To

" To take thee to my home I sware,
" And here we were to meet:
" Wilt thou a narrow coffin share,
" And part my winding-sheet?

" But late the lord of many lands,
" And now a grave is all:
" My blood is warm upon his hands
" Who revels in my hall.

" Yet think thy father's hoary hair
" Is water'd with his tears;
" He has but thee to sooth his care,
" And prop his load of years.

" Remember Edward when he's gone,
" He only liv'd for thee;
" And when thou'rt pensive, and alone,
" O Marg'ret call on me!

" Yet

" Yet deep beneath the mould'ring clod

  " I reſt my wounded head;

" And terrible that call, and loud,

  " Which ſhall awake the dead."

" No, Edward, I will follow thee,

  " And ſhare thy hapleſs doom :

" Companions ſhall our ſpirits be,

  " Tho' diſtant is thy tomb.

" O ! never to my father's tower

  " Will I return again !

" A bleeding heart has little power

  " To eaſe another's pain.

" Upon the wing my ſpirit flies,

  " I feel my courſe is run ;

" Nor ſhall theſe dim and weary eyes

  " Behold to-morrow's ſun."

Like

Like early dew, or hoary froſt,
 Spent with the beaming day,
So ſhrunk the pale and wat'ry ghoſt,
 And dimly wore away.

No longer Marg'ret felt the ſtorm,
 She bow'd her lovely head;
And with her lover's fleeting form,
 Her gentle ſpirit fled.

PART

PART II.

———

" LOUD roars the wind that ſhakes this wall;

   " It is no common blaſt:

" Deep hollow ſounds paſs thro' my hall,

   " O would the night were paſt!

" Methinks the dæmons of the air

   " Upon the turrets growl;

" While down the empty winding ſtair

   " Their deep'ning murmurs roll.

" The glimm'ring fire cheers not the gloom:

   " How blue its weakly ray!

" And like a taper in a tomb,

   " But ſpreads the more diſmay.

                " Athwart

" Athwart its melancholy light
 " The lengthen'd ſhadow falls :
" My grandſires, to my troubled ſight,
 " Low'r on me from theſe walls.

" Methinks yon angry warrior's head
 " Doth in its caſement frown,
" And darts a look, as if it ſaid,
 " Where haſt thou laid my ſon ?

" But will theſe fancies never ceaſe ?
 " O, would the night were run !
" My troubled ſoul can find no peace,
 " But with the morning ſun.

" Vain hope ! the guilty never reſt ;
 " Diſmay is always near :
" There is a midnight in the breaſt
 " No morn ſhall ever cheer.

       " Tʰe

" The weary hind is now at reſt,

   " Tho' lowly is his head,

" How ſweetly lies the guiltleſs breaſt,

   " Upon the hardeſt bed!

" The beggar, in his wretched haunt,

   " May now a monarch be ;

" Forget his woe, forget his want,

   " For all can ſleep but me.

" I've dar'd whate'er the boldeſt can,

   " Then why this childiſh dread ;

" I never fear'd a living man,

   " And ſhall I fear the dead !

" No, whiſtling ſtorms may ſhake my tower,

   " And paſſing ſpirits ſcream :

" Their ſhadowy arms are void of power,

   " And but a gloomy dream.

                          " But,

" But, lo ! a form advancing flow
  " Acrofs my dufky hall !
" Art thou a friend ? art thou a foe ?
  " O, anfwer to my call !"

Still nearer to the glimm'ring light
  The tow'ring figure ftrode,
Till full, and horrid to the fight,
  The murther'd Edward ftood.

His hand a broken dagger fway'd,
  Like Time's dark threat'ning dart ;
And pointed to the rugged blade
  That quiver'd in his heart.

The blood ftill trickled from his head,
  And clotted was his hair,
That on his manly fhoulders fpread ;
  His mangled breaft was bare.

His

His face was like the muddy fky
    Before the coming fnow;
And dark and dreadful was his eye,
    And cloudy was his brow.

Pale Conrad fhrunk, but grafp'd his fword;
    Fear thrill'd in ev'ry vein;
His quiv'ring lip half-fpoke its word;
    He paus'd, and fhrunk again.

" Pale bloody fpectre, at this hour
    " Why do'ft thou haunt the night?
" Has the deep gloomy vault no power
    " To keep thee from my fight?

" Why do'ft thou glare? Why do'ft thou wave
    " That fatal curfed knife?
" The deed is done, and from the grave
    " Who can recall to life?

                                    " Why

" Why rolls thine eye beneath thy brow,

" Dark as the midnight ſtorm?

" What do'ſt thou want? O, let me know!

" But hide thy dreadful form.

" I'd give the life's blood from my heart

" To waſh my crime away:

" If thou'rt a ſpirit, O, depart!

" Nor haunt a wretch of clay.

" Say, do'ſt thou with the bleſſed dwell?

" Return and bleſſed be!

" Or com'ſt thou from the loweſt hell?

" I am more curſt than thee."

The form advanc'd with ſolemn ſtep,

As though it meant to ſpeak;

And thrice it mov'd its mutt'ring lip,

But ſilence did not break.

Then

Then sternly stalk'd with heavy pace,
  Which shook the trembling wall;
And, frowning, turn'd its angry face,
  And vanish'd from the hall.

With fixed eyes, pale Conrad stood,
  That from their sockets swell;
Back on his heart ran the cold blood,
  He shudder'd as he fell.

Night fled, and thro' the window 'gan
  The early light to play;
But on a more unhappy man
  Ne'er shone the dawning day.

The gladsome sun all nature cheers,
  But cannot charm his cares:
Still dwells his mind with gloomy fears,
  And murther'd Edward glares.

                              PART

PART III.

———

" No reſt nor comfort can I find,

  " I watch the midnight hour;

" I ſit and liſten to the wind

  " Which beats upon my tower.

" Methinks low voices from the ground

  " Break mournful on mine ear,

" And thro' theſe empty chambers ſound

  " So diſmal and ſo drear.

" The ghoſt of ſome departed friend

  " Doth in my ſorrows ſhare;

" Or is it but the ruſhing wind

  " That mocketh my deſpair.

E

" Sad

" Sad thro' the hall the pale lamp gleams
　　" Upon my father's arms :
" My foul is fill'd with gloomy dreams,
　　" I fear unknown alarms.

" Oh ! I have known this lonely place
　　" With ev'ry bleſſing ſtor'd ;
" And many a friend with cheerful face
　　" Sit ſmiling at my board,

" Whilſt round the fire, in early bloom,
　　" My harmleſs children play'd,
" Who now within the narrow tomb
　　" Are with their mother laid.

" And now low bends my wretched head,
　　" And thoſe I lov'd are gone :
" My friends, my family, all are fled,
　　" And I am left alone.

　　　　　　　　　　　　　　" Oft'

" Oft' as the cheerlefs fire declines,

    " In it I fadly trace,

" As 'lone I fit, the half form'd lines

    " Of many a much lov'd face.

" But chief, O Marg'ret! to my mind

    " Thy lovely features rife:

" I ftrive to think thee lefs unkind,

    " And wipe my ftreaming eyes.

" For only thee I had to vaunt,

    " Thou wert thy mother's pride:

" She left thee like a fhooting plant

    " To fcreen my widow'd fide.

" But thou haft, left me weak, forlorn,

    " And chill'd with age's froft,

" To count my weary days, and mourn

    " The comforts I have loft.

 Unkindly

" Unkindly fair ! why did'ft thou go ?

  " O, had I known the truth !

" Tho' Edward's father was my foe,

  " I would have blefs'd the youth.

" O could I fee that face again,

  " Whofe fmile calm'd ev'ry ftrife !

" And hear that voice, which footh'd my pain,

  " And made me wifh for life !

" Thy harp hangs filent by the wall :

  " My nights are fad and long :

" And thou art in a diftant hall,

  " Where ftrangers raife the fong.

" Ha ! fome delufion of the mind

  " My fenfes doth confound !

" It was the harp, and not the wind,

  " That did fo fweetly found."

Old

Old Arno rofe, all wan as death,
   With broken fteps of care;
And oft' he check'd his quick-heav'd breath,
   And turn'd his eager ear.

When like a full, but diftant choir
   The fwelling found return'd;
And with the foft and trembling wire,
   The fighing echoes mourn'd.

Then foftly whifper'd o'er the fong
   Which Marg'ret lov'd to play,
Like fome fweet dirge, and fad, and long,
   It faintly died away.

His dim-worn eyes to heav'n he caft,
   Where all his griefs were known;
And fmote upon his troubled breaft,
   And heav'd a heavy groan.

E 3

" I know

" I know it is my daughter's hand,

   " But 'tis no hand of clay :

" And here a lonely wretch I ſtand,

    " All childleſs, bent, and grey.

" And art thou low, my lovely child ?

    " And haſt thou met thy doom ?

" And has thy flatt'ring morning ſmil'd,

    " To lead but to the tomb ?

" O let me ſee thee ere we part,

    " For ſouls like thine are bleſt ;

" O let me fold thee to my heart

    " If aught of form thou haſt.

" This paſſing miſt enrobes thy charms :

    " Alas, to nought 'tis ſhrunk !

" And hollow ſtrike my empty arms

    " Againſt my aged trunk.

                       " Thou'rt

" Thou'rt fled like the low ev'ning breath

   " That sighs upon the hill :

" O stay ! tho' in thy weeds of death,

   " Thou art my daughter still."

Loud wak'd the sound, then fainter grew,

   And long and sadly mourn'd ;

And softly sigh'd a long adieu,

   And never more return'd.

Old Arno stretch'd him on the ground,

   Thick as the gloom of night,

Death's misty shadows gather'd round,

   And swam before his sight.

He heav'd a deep and deadly groan,

   Which rent his lab'ring breast ;

And long before the morning shone,

   His spirit was at rest.

E 4   A REVERIE.

A R E V E R I E.

BESIDE a fpreading elm, from whofe high boughs
Like knotted tufts the crow's light dwelling fhows,
Where fcreen'd from northern blafts, and winter
   proof,
Snug ftands the parfon's barn with thatched roof;
At chaff-ftrew'd door, where, in the morning ray,
The gilded mots in mazy circles play,
And fleepy Comrade in the fun is laid,
More grateful to the cur than neighb'ring fhade;
In fnowy fhirt unbrac'd, brown Robin ftood,
And leant upon his flail in thoughtful mood:
His full round cheek where deeper flufhes glow,
The dewy drops which gliften on his brow;

His

His dark cropt pate that erſt at church or fair,

So ſmooth and ſilky, ſhew'd his morning's care,

Which all uncouth in matted locks combin'd,

Now, ends erect, defies the ruffling wind;

His neck-band looſe, and hoſen rumpled low,

A careful lad, nor ſlack at labour ſhew.

Nor ſcraping chickens chirping 'mongſt the ſtraw,

Nor croaking rook o'er-head, nor chatt'ring daw;

Loud-breathing cow amongſt the rampy weeds,

Nor grunting ſow that in the furrow feeds;

Nor ſudden breeze that ſhakes the quaking leaves,

And lightly ruſtles thro' the ſcatter'd ſheaves;

Nor floating ſtraw that ſkims athwart his noſe,

The deeply muſing youth may diſcompoſe.

For Nelly fair, and blytheſt village maid,

Whoſe tuneful voice beneath the hedge-row ſhade,

At early milking, o'er the meadows born,

E'er cheer'd the ploughman's toil at riſing morn:

The neateſt maid that e'er, in linen gown,

Bore cream and butter to the market town:

The

The tighteſt laſs, that with untutor'd air
E'er footed ale-houſe floor at wake or fair,
Since Eaſter laſt had Robin's heart poſſeſt,
And many a time diſturb'd his nightly reſt.
Full oft' returning from the loofen'd plough,
He ſlack'd his pace, and knit his thoughtful brow;
And oft' ere half his threſher's taſk was o'er,
Would muſe, with arms acroſs, at cooling door:
His mind thus bent, with downcaſt eyes he ſtood,
And leant upon his flail in thoughtful mood.
His ſoul o'er many a ſoft rememb'rance ran,
And, mutt'ring to himſelf, the youth began.

" Ah! happy is the man whoſe early lot
" Hath made him maſter of a furniſh'd cot;
" Who trains the vine that round his window
" grows,
" And after ſetting ſun his garden hoes;
" Whoſe wattled pales his own encioſure ſhield,
" Who toils not daily in another's field.

" Where'er

" Where'er he goes, to church or market town,

" With more refpect he and his dog are known :

" A brifker face he wears at wake or fair,

" Nor views with longing eyes the pedlar's ware,

" But buys at will or ribands, gloves, or beads,

" And willing maidens to the ale-houfe leads :

" And, Oh ! fecure from toils which cumber life,

" He makes the maid he loves an eafy wife.

" Ah, Nelly ! can'ft thou with contented mind,

" Become the help-mate of a lab'ring hind,

" And fhare his lot, whate'er the chances be,

" Who hath no dow'r, but love, to fix on thee?

" Yes, gayeft maid may meekeft matron prove,

" And things of little note may 'token love.

" When from the church thou cam'ft at eventide

" And I and red-hair'd Sufan by thy fide,

" I pull'd the bloffoms from the bending tree,

" And fome to Sufan gave, and fome to thee;

" Thine were the beft, and well thy fmiling eye

" The diff'rence mark'd, and guefs'd the reafon why.

" When on a holy-day we rambling ftray'd,

" And pafs'd old Hodge's cottage in the glade;

" Neat was the garden drefs'd, fweet hum'd the
    " bee,

" I wifh'd both cot and Nelly made for me;

" And well methought thy very eyes reveal'd

" The felf-fame wifh within thy breaft conceal'd.

" When artful, once, I fought my love to tell,

" And fpoke to thee of one who lov'd thee well,

" You faw the cheat, and jeering homeward hied,

" Yet fecret pleafure in thy looks I fpied.

" Ay, gayeft maid may meekeft matron prove,

" And fmaller figns than thefe have 'token'd love."

Now, at a diftance, on the neighb'ring plain,
With creaking wheels flow comes the heavy wain:
High on its tow'ring load a maid appears,
And Nelly's voice founds fhrill in Robin's ears.
Quick from his hand he throws the cumb'rous flail,
And leaps with lightfome limbs th' enclofing pale.

O'er

O'er field and fence he fcours, and furrow wide,

With waken'd Comrade barking by his fide;

Whilft tracks of trodden grain, and fidelong hay,

And broken hedge-flow'rs fweet, mark his impetuous

   way

A DIS-

A DISAPPOINTMENT.

ON village green, whofe fmooth and well worn fod,
Crofs-path'd with every goffip's foot is trod;
By cottage door where playful children run,
And cats and curs fit bafking in the fun :
Where o'er the earthen feat the thorn is bent,
Crofs-arm'd, and back to wall, poor William leant.
His bonnet broad drawn o'er his gather'd brow,
His hanging lip and lengthen'd vifage fhew
A mind but ill at eafe. With motions ftrange,
His liftlefs limbs their wayward poftures change;
Whilft many a crooked line and curious maze,
With clouted fhoon, he on the fand pourtrays.
The half-chew'd ftraw fell flowly from his mouth,
And to himfelf low mutt'ring fpoke the youth.

" How

" How simple is the lad ! and reft of skill,

" Who thinks with love to fix a woman's will:

" Who ev'ry Sunday morn, to please her sight,

" Knots up his neck-cloth gay, and hosen white:

" Who for her pleasure keeps his pockets bare,

" And half his wages spends on pedlar's ware;

" When every niggard clown, or dotard old,

" Who hides in secret nooks his oft told gold,

" Whose field or orchard tempts with all her pride,

" At little cost may win her for his bride ;

" Whilst all the meed her silly lover gains

" Is but the neighbours' jeering for his pains.

" On Sunday last when Susan's bands were read,

" And I astonish'd sat with hanging head,

" Cold grew my shrinking limbs, and loose my knee,

" Whilst every neighbour's eye was fix'd on me.

" Ah, Sue ! when last we work'd at Hodge's hay,

" And still at me you jeer'd in wanton play ;

" When last at fair, well pleas'd by show-man's stand,

" You took the new-bought fairing from my hand;

" When

" When at old Hobb's you fung that fong fo gay,

" Sweet William ftill the burthen of the lay,

" I little thought, alas! the lots were caft,

" That thou fhou'd'ft be another's bride at laft:

" And had, when laft we trip'd it on the green

" And laugh'd at ftiff-back'd Rob, fmall thought I

    " ween,

" Ere yet another fcanty month was flown,

" To fee thee wedded to the hateful clown.

" Ay, lucky fwain, more gold thy pockets line;

" But did thefe fhapely limbs refemble thine,

" I'd ftay at home, and tend the houfehold geer,

" Nor on the green with other lads appear.

" Ay, lucky fwain, no ftore thy cottage lacks,

" And round thy barn thick ftands the fhelter'd

    " ftacks;

" But did fuch features hard my vifage grace,

" I'd never budge the bonnet from my face.

" Yet let it be: it fhall not break my eafe:

" He beft deferves who doth the maiden pleafe.

" Such

" Such filly caufe no more fhall give me pain,

" Nor ever maiden crofs my reft again.

" Such grizzly fuitors with their tafte agree,

" And the black fiend may take them all for me !

Now thro' the village rife confufed founds,

Hoarfe lads, and children fhrill, and yelping hounds.

Straight ev'ry matron at the door is feen,

And paufing hedgers on their mattocks lean.

At every narrow lane, and alley mouth,

Loud laughing laffes ftand, and joking youth.

A near approaching band in colours gay,

With minftrels blythe before to cheer the way,

From clouds of curling duft which onward fly,

In rural fplendour break upon the eye.

As in their way they hold fo gayly on,

Caps, beads, and buttons glancing in the fun,

Each village wag, with eye of roguifh caft,

Some maiden jogs, and vents the ready jeft;

Whilft

Whilft village toafts the paffing belles deride,

And fober matrons marvel at their pride.

But William, head erect, with fettled brow,

In fullen filence view'd the paffing fhew;

And oft' he fcratch'd his pate with manful grace,

And fcorn'd to pull the bonnet o'er his face:

But did with fteady look unmoved wait,

Till hindmoft man had turn'd the church-yard gate;

Then turn'd him to his cot with vifage flat,

Where honeft Tray upon the threfhold fat.

Up jump'd the kindly beaft his hand to lick,

And, for his pains, receiv'd an angry kick.

Loud fhuts the flapping door with thund'ring din;

The echoes round their circling courfe begin,

From cot to cot, in wide progreffive fwell,

Deep groans the church-yard wall and neighb'ring dell,

And Tray, refponfive, joins with long and piteous yell.

A LAMENT-

A LAMENTATION.

WHERE ancient broken wall enclofes round,
From tread of lawlefs feet, the hallow'd ground,
And fomber yews their dewy branches wave
O'er many a motey ftone and mounded grave:
Where parifh church, confus'dly to the fight,
With deeper darknefs prints the fhades of night,
And mould'ring tombs uncouthly gape around,
And rails and fallen ftones beftrew the ground;
In loofen'd garb derang'd, with fcatter'd hair,
His bofom open to the nightly air,
Lone, o'er a new heap'd grave poor Bafil bent,
And to himfelf began his fimple plaint.

" Alas! how cold thy home! how low thou art!
" Who wert the pride and miftrefs of my heart.

　　　　　　　　" The

" The fallen leaves light ruſtling o'er thee paſs,

" And o'er thee waves the rank and dewy graſs.

" The new laid ſods in decent order tell

" How narrow now the ſpace where thou muſt dwell.

" Now rough and wint'ry winds may on thee beat,

" And drizzly drifting ſnow, and ſummer's heat;

" Each paſſing ſeaſon rub, for woe is me!

" Or ſtorm, or ſunſhine, is the ſame to thee.

" Ah, Mary! lovely was thy ſlender form,

" And ſweet thy cheerful brow, that knew no ſtorm.

" Thy ſteps were graceful on the village-green,

" As tho' thou had'ſt ſome courtly lady been:

" At church or market, ſtill the gayeſt laſs,

" Each younker ſlack'd his ſpeed to ſee thee paſs.

" At early milking, tuneful was thy lay,

" And ſweet thy homeward ſong at cloſe of day;

" But ſweeter far, and ev'ry youth's deſire,

" Thy cheerful converſe by the ev'ning fire.

" Alas! no more thou'lt foot the graſſy ſward!

" No ſong of thine ſhall ever more be heard!

" Yet

" Yet now they trip it lightly on the green,

" As blythe and gay as thou hadſt never been:

" The careleſs younker whiſtles lightſome by,

" And other maidens catch his roving eye:

" Around the ev'ning fire, with little care,

" The neighbours ſit, and ſcarcely miſs thee there;

" And when the night advancing darkens round,

" They to their reſt retire, and ſlumber found.

" But Baſil cannot reſt; his days are ſad,

" And long his nights upon the weary bed.

" Yet ſtill in broken dreams thy form appears,

" And ſtill my boſom proves a lover's fears.

" I guide thy footſteps thro' the tangled wood;

" I catch thee ſinking in the boiſt'rous flood;

" I ſhield thy boſom from the threaten'd ſtroke;

" I claſp thee falling from the headlong rock;

" But ere we reach the dark and dreadful deep,

" High heaves my troubled breaſt, I wake, and weep.

" At ev'ry wailing of the midnight wind

" Thy lowly dwelling comes into my mind.

F 3   " When

" When rain beats on my roof, wild storms abroad,

" I think upon thy bare and beaten sod;

" I hate the comfort of a shelter'd home,

" And hie me forth o'er fenceless fields to roam:

" I leave the paths of men for dreary waste,

" And bare my forehead to the howling blast.

" O Mary! loss of thee hath fix'd my doom:

" This world around me is a weary gloom:

" Dull heavy musings down my spirits weigh,

" I cannot sleep by night, nor work by day.

" Or wealth or pleasure floweth minds inspire,

" But cheerless is their toil who nought desire.

" Let happier friends divide my farmers' stock,

" Cut down my grain, and sheer my little flock;

" For now my only care on earth shall be

" Here ev'ry Sunday morn to visit thee;

" And in the holy church, with heart sincere,

" And humble mind, our worthy curate hear:

" He best can tell, when earthly cares are past,

" The surest way to meet with thee at last.

" I'll

" I'll thus a while a weary life abide,

" Till wasting Time hath laid me by thy side;

" For now on earth there is no place for me,

" Nor peace, nor flumber, till I reft with thee."

Loud, from the lofty fpire, with piercing knell,

Solemn, and awful, toll'd the parifh bell;

A later hour than ruftics deem it meet

That church-yard ground be trode by mortal feet,

The wailing lover ftartled at the found,

And rais'd his head and caft his eyes around.

The gloomy pile in ftrengthen'd horrour lower'd,

Large and majeftic ev'ry object tower'd:

Dim thro' the gloom they fhew'd their forms unknown,

And tall and ghaftly rofe each whiten'd ftone:

Aloft the waking fcreech-owl 'gan to fing,

And paft him fkim'd the bat with flapping wing.

The fears of nature woke within his breaft;

He left the hallowed fpot of Mary's reft,

F 4   And

And fped his way the church-yard wall to gain,

Then check'd his coward heart, and turn'd again.

The fhadows round a deeper horrour wear;

A deeper filence hangs upon his ear;

A ftiller reft is o'er the fettled fcene;

His flutt'ring heart recoils, and fhrinks again.

With hafty fteps he meafures back the ground,

And leaps with fummon'd force the church-yard bound;

Then home with knocking limbs, and quicken'd breath,

His footftep urges from the place of death,

AN

AN ADDRESS TO THE MUSES.

Y E tuneful Sisters of the lyre,
Who dreams and fantasies inspire;
Who over poesy preside,
And on a lofty hill abide
Above the ken of mortal sight,
Fain would I sing of you, could I address ye right.

Thus known, your pow'r of old was sung,
And temples with your praises rung;
And when the song of battle rose,
Or kindling wine, or lovers' woes,
The poet's spirit inly burn'd,
And still to you his upcast eyes were turn'd.

The

The youth all wrapp'd in vision bright,
Beheld your robes of flowing white:
And knew your forms benignly grand,
An awful, but a lovely band;
And felt your inspiration strong,
And warmly pour'd his rapid lay along.

The aged bard all heav'n-ward glow'd,
And hail'd you daughters of a god:
Tho' to his dimmer eyes were seen
Nor graceful form, nor heav'nly mien,
Full well he felt that ye were near,
And heard you in the blast that shook his hoary hair.

Ye lighten'd up the valley's bloom,
And deeper spread the forest's gloom;
The lofty hill sublimer stood,
And grander rose the mighty flood;
For then Religion lent her aid,
And o'er the mind of man your sacred empire spread.

Tho'

Tho' rolling ages now are paft,

And altars low, and temples wafte;

Tho' rites and oracles are o'er,

And gods and heros rule no more;

Your fading honours ftill remain,

And ftill your vot'ries call, a long and motley train.

They feek you not on hill and plain,

Nor court you in the facred fane;

Nor meet you in the mid-day dream,

Upon the bank of hallowed ftream;

Yet ftill for infpiration fue,

And ftill each lifts his fervent prayer to you.

He knows ye not in woodland gloom,

But wooes ye in the fhelfed room;

And feeks you in the dufty nook,

And meets you in the letter'd book;

Full well he knows you by your names,

And ftill with poets faith your prefence claims.

The

The youthful poet, pen in hand,
All by the fide of blotted ftand,
In rev'rie deep, which none may break,
Sits rubbing of his beardlefs cheek;
And well his infpiration knows,
E'en by the dewy drops that trickle o'er his nofe.

The tuneful fage of riper fame,
Perceives you not in heated frame;
But at conclufion of his verfe,
Which ftill his mutt'ring lips rehearfe,
Oft' waves his hand in grateful pride,
And owns the heav'nly pow'r that did his fancy guide.

O lovely fifters! is it true,
That they are all infpir'd by you?
And while they write, with magic charm'd,
And high enthufiafm warm'd,
We may not queftion heav'nly lays,
For well I wot, they give you all the praife.

O lovely

O lovely fifters ! well it fhews
How wide and far your bounty flows :
Then why from me withhold your beams ?
Unvifited of heav'nly dreams,
Whene'er I aim at heights fublime,
Still downward am I call'd to feek fome ftubborn rhyme.

No hafty lightning breaks the gloom,
Nor flafhing thoughts unfought for come,
Nor fancies wake in time of need ;
I labour much with little fpeed ;
And when my ftudied tafk is done,
Too well, alas ! I mark it for my own.

Yet fhould you never fmile on me,
And rugged ftill my verfes be ;
Unpleafing to the tuneful train,
Who only prize a flowing ftrain ;
And ftill the learned fcorn my lays,
I'll lift my heart to you, and fing your praife.

Your

Your varied miniſtry to trace,

Your honour'd names, and godlike race;

And lofty bow'rs where fountains flow,

They'll better ſing who better know;

I praiſe ye not with Grecian lyre,

Nor will I hail ye daughters of a heathen fire.

Ye are the ſpirits who preſide

In earth, and air, and ocean wide;

In hiſſing flood, and crackling fire;

In horror dread, and tumult dire;

In ſtilly calm, and ſtormy wind,

And rule the anſw'ring changes in the human mind.

High on the tempeſt-beaten hill,

Your miſty ſhapes ye ſhift at will;

The wild fantaſtic clouds ye form;

Your voice is in the midnight ſtorm,

Whilſt in the dark and lonely hour,

Oft' ſtarts the boldeſt heart, and owns your ſecret pow'r.

From

From you, when growling storms are paſt,

And light'ning ceaſes on the waſte,

And when the ſcene of blood is o'er,

And groans of death are heard no more,

Still holds the mind each parted form,

Like after echoing of th' o'erpaſſed ſtorm.

When cloſing glooms o'erſpread the day,

And what we love has paſs'd away,

Ye kindly bid each pleaſing ſcene

Within the boſom ſtill remain,

Like moons who doth their watches run

With the reflected brightneſs of the parted ſun.

The ſhining day, and nightly ſhade,

The cheerful plain and gloomy glade,

The homeward flocks, and ſhepherds play,

The buſy hamlet's cloſing day,

Full many a breaſt with pleaſures ſwell,

Who ne'er ſhall have the gift of words to tell.

Oft'

Oft' when the moon looks from on high,

And black around the fhadows lie;

And bright the fparkling waters gleam,

And rufhes ruftle by the ftream,

Shrill founds, and fairy forms are known

By fimple 'nighted fwains, who wander late alone.

Ye kindle up the inward glow,

Ye ftrengthen ev'ry outward fhow;

Ye overleap the ftrongeft bar,

And join what Nature funders far:

And vifit oft' in fancies wild,

The breaft of learned fage, and fimple child.

From him who wears a monarch's crown,

To the unletter'd artlefs clown,

All in fome ftrange and lonely hour

Have felt, unfought, your fecret pow'r,

And lov'd your roving fancies well,

You add but to the bard the art to tell.

Ye

Ye mighty ſpirits of the ſong,

To whom the poets' pray'rs belong,

My lowly boſom to inſpire,

And kindle with your ſacred fire,

Your wild obſcuring heights to brave,

Is boon, alas! too great for me to crave.

But O, ſuch ſenſe of matter bring!

As they who feel and never ſing

Wear on their hearts, it will avail

With ſimple words to tell my tale;

And ſtill contented will I be,

Tho' greater inſpirations never fall to me.

G   A ME-

A MELANCHOLY LOVER's FARE-
WELL TO HIS MISTRESS.

MY Phillis, all my hopes are o'er,
And I fhall fee thy face no more.
Since ev'ry fecret wifh is vain,
I will not ftay to give thee pain.
Then do not hang thy low'ring brow,
But let me blefs thee ere I go :
Nor, O, defpife my laft adieu !
I've lov'd thee long, and lov'd thee true.

The profpects of my youth are croft,
My health is flown, my vigour loft;
My foothing friends augment my pain,
And cheerlefs is my native plain ;

Dark

Dark o'er my ſpirit hangs the gloom,

And thy diſdain has fix'd my doom.

But light gales ruffle o'er the ſea,

Which ſoon ſhall bear me far from thee;

And whereſoe'er our courſe is caſt,

I know will bear me to my reſt.

Full deep beneath the briny wave,

Where reſt the venturous and brave,

A place may be decreed for me;

And ſhould no tempeſt raiſe the ſea,

Far hence upon a foreign land,

Whoſe ſons, perhaps, with friendly hand

The ſtranger's lowly tomb may raiſe;

A broken heart will end my days.

But Heaven's bleſſing on thee reſt!

And may no troubles vex thy breaſt!

Perhaps, when penſive and alone,

You'll think of me when I am gone;

And

And gentle tears of pity fhed,
When I am in my narrow bed.
Yet foftly let thy forrow flow!
And greater may'ft thou never know!
All free from worldly care and ftrife,
Long may'ft thou live a happy life!
And ev'ry earthly bleffing find,
Thou lovelieft of womankind:
And bleft thy fecret wifhes be!
Tho' cruel thou haft been to me.

And do'ft thou then thine arm extend
And may I take thy lovely hand?
And do thine eyes thus gently look,
As tho' fome kindly wifh they fpoke?
My gentle Phillis, tho' fevere,
I do not grudge the ills I bear;
But ftill my greateft grief will be,
To think my love has troubled thee.

O, do

O, do not fcorn this fwelling grief!

The laden bofom feeks relief:

Nor yet this infant weaknefs blame,

For thou haft made me what I am.

But hark! the failors call away,

No longer may I ling'ring ftay;

May peace within thy manfion dwell!

O, gentle Phillis, fare thee well!

A CHEER-

A CHEERFUL TEMPERED LOVER'S FAREWELL TO HIS MISTRESS.

THE light winds on the ſtreamers play
That ſoon ſhall bear me far away;
My comrades give the parting cheer,
And I alone have linger'd here.
Now Phill. my love, ſince it will be,
And I muſt bid farewell to thee,
Since ev'ry hope of thee is flown,
Ne'er ſend me from thee with a frown;
But let me kindly take thy hand,
And bid God bleſs me in a foreign land.

No

No more I'll loiter by thy fide,

Well pleas'd thy gamefome taunts to bide;

Nor lovers' gambols lightly try

To make me graceful in thine eye;

Nor fing the merry roundelay,

To cheer thee at the clofe of day.

Yet ne'erthelefs tho' we muft part,

I'll bear thee ftill upon my heart;

And oft' I'll fill the ruddy glafs,

To toaft my lovely fcornful lafs.

Far hence, upon a foreign fhore,

Still will I keep an open door,

And ftill my little fortune fhare

With all who ever breath'd my native air.

And who thy beauteous face hath feen,

Or ever near thy dwelling been,

Shall pufh about the flowing bowl,

And be the mafter of the whole.

And ev'ry woman for thy fake,

Though proud and cruel, as they're weak,

G 4   Shall

Shall in my walls protection find,
Thou faireſt of a fickle kind.

O, dearly! dearly! have I paid,
Thou little haughty cruel maid,
To give that inward peace to thee,
Which thou haſt ta'en away from me.
Soft haſt thou ſlept, with boſom light,
Whilſt I have watch'd the weary night;
And now I croſs the ſurgy deep,
That thou may'ſt ſtill untroubled ſleep—
But in thine eyes, what do I ſee,
That looks as tho' they pitied me?
I thank thee, Phill. yet be not ſad,
I leave no blame upon thy head.
I would, more grac'd with pleaſing make,
I had been better for thy ſake,
But yet, perhaps, when I ſhall dwell
Far hence, thou'lt ſometimes think how well—

I dare

I dare not ſtay, ſince we muſt part,
T''expoſe a fond and fooliſh heart;
Where'er I go, it beats for you,
God bleſs ye, Phill. adieu! adieu!

A PROUD

A PROUD LOVER'S FAREWELL
TO HIS MISTRESS.

FAREWELL thou haughty, cruel fair !
Upon thy brow no longer wear
That fombre look of cold difdain,
Thou ne'er fhalt fee my face again.
Now ev'ry filly wifh is o'er,
And fears and doubtings are no more.

All cruel as thou art to me,
Long has my heart been fix'd on thee ;
On thee I've mus'd the live-long day,
And thought the weary night away ;
I've trac'd thy footfteps o'er the green,
And fhar'd thy rambles oft unfeen ;

I've

I've linger'd near thee night and day,
When thou haft thought me far away;
I've watch'd the turning of thy face,
And fondly mark'd thy moving grace;
And wept thy rifing fmiles to fee;
I've been a fool for love of thee.

Yet do not think I ftay the while
Thy weakly pity to beguile:
Let forced favour fruitlefs prove!
The pity curft, that brings not love!
No woman e'er fhall give me pain,
Or ever break my reft again:
Nor aught that comes of woman kind
Have pow'r again to move my mind.

Far on a foreign fhore I'll feek
Some lonely ifland, bare and bleak;
I'll feek fome wild and rugged cell,
And with untamed creatures dwell.
To hear their cries is now my choice,
Far more than man's deceitful voice:

To

To liſten to the howling wind,
Than luring tongue of womankind.
They look not beautiful and good,
But roughſome ſeem as they are rude.

  O Phillis ! thou haſt wreck'd a heart,
Which proudly bears, but feels the ſmart.
Adieu ! adieu ! ſhould'ſt thou e'er prove
The pang of ill-requited love,
Thou'lt know what I have borne for thee,
And then thou wilt remember me.

                       A POET,

A POET, OR, SOUND-HEARTED LOVER'S FAREWELL TO HIS MISTRESS.

Fair Nymph, who doſt my fate controul,
And reign'ſt the miſtreſs of my ſoul,
Where thou all bright in beauties ray
Haſt held a long tyrannick ſway,
They who the hardeſt rule maintain,
In their commands do ſtill refrain
From what impoſſible muſt prove,
But thou haſt bade me ceaſe to love;
Nor would ſome gentle mercy give,
And only bid me ceaſe to live.

Ah !

Ah! when the magnet's pow'r is o'er,

The compass then will point no more;

And when no verdure cloaths the spring,

The tuneful birds forget to sing:

But thou all sweet and heav'nly fair,

Hast bade thy swain from love forbear.

In pity let thine own fair hand

A death's-wound to this bosom send:

This tender heart of purest faith

May then resign thee with its breath;

And in the sun-beam of thine eye

A proud and willing victim die.

But since thou wilt not have it so,

Far from thy presence will I go:

Far from my heart's dear bliss I'll stray,

Since I no longer can obey.

In foreign climes I'll distant roam,

No more to hail my native home:

To

To foreign fwains I'll pour my woe,
In foreign plains my tears fhall flow:
By murm'ring ftream and fhady grove
Shall other echoes tell my love;
And richer flow'rs of vivid hue
Upon my tomb fhall other maidens ftrew.

Adieu, dear Phillis! fhould'ft thou e'er
Some foft and plaintive ftory hear,
Of haplefs youth who died for love,
Or all forlorn did banifh'd rove,
O think of me! nor then deny
The gentle tribute of a figh.

It may be objected that all thefe lovers are equally
fad, though one is a cheerful, the other a melancholy
lover. It is true they are all equally fad, for they are
all equally in love, and in defpair, when it is impof-
fible for them to be otherwife; but if I have pictured
their

their farewell complaints in fuch a way as to give you an idea that one lover is naturally of a melancholy, one of a cheerful, and one of a proud temper, I have done all that is intended.

THE

THE STORM-BEAT MAID.

SOMEWHAT AFTER THE STYLE OF OUR OLD
ENGLISH BALLADS.

ALL fhrouded in the winter fnow,
   The maiden held her way;
Nor chilly winds that roughly blow,
   Nor dark night could her ftay.

O'er hill and dale, through bufh and briar,
   She on her journey kept;
Save often when fhe 'gan to tire,
   She ftop'd awhile and wept.

Wild creatures left their caverns drear,
   To raife their nightly yell;
But little doth the bofom fear,
   Where inward troubles dwell.

H   No

No watch-light from the diſtant ſpire,
　　To cheer the gloom ſo deep,
Nor twinkling ſtar, nor cottage fire
Did thro' the darkneſs peep.

Yet heedleſs ſtill ſhe held her way,
　　Nor fear'd ſhe crag nor dell;
Like ghoſt that thro' the gloom to ſtray,
Wakes with the midnight bell.

Now night thro' her dark watches ran,
　　Which lock the peaceful mind;
And thro' the neighb'ring hamlets 'gan
　　To wake the yawning hind.

Yet bark of dog, nor village cock,
　　That ſpoke the morning near;
Nor gray-light trembling on the rock,
　　Her 'nighted mind could cheer.

The

The whirling flail, and clacking mill
   Wake with the early day;
And carelefs children, loud and fhrill,
   With new-made fnow-balls play.

And as fhe pafs'd each cottage door,
They did their gambols ceafe;
And old men fhook their locks fo hoar,
   And wifh'd her fpirit peace.

For fometimes flow, and fometimes faft,
   She held her wav'ring pace;
Like early fpring's inconftant blaft,
   That ruffles evening's face.

At length with weary feet fhe came,
   Where in a fhelt'ring wood,
Whofe mafter bore no humble name,
A ftately caftle ftood.

The

The open gate, and fmoking fires,
  Which cloud the air fo thin;
And fhrill bell tinkling from the fpires,
  Befpoke a feaft within.

With bufy looks, and hafty tread,
  The fervants crofs the hall;
And many a page, in bufkins red,
  Await the mafter's call.

Fair ftreaming bows of bridal white
  On ev'ry fhoulder play'd;
And clean, in lily kerchief dight,
  Trip'd every houfhold maid.

She afk'd for neither lord nor dame,
  Nor who the manfion own'd;
But ftraight into the hall fhe came,
  And fat her on the ground.

The

The buſy crew all crouded nigh,
　And round the ſtranger ſtar'd ;
But ſtill ſhe roll'd her wand'ring eye,
　Nor for their queſtions car'd.

" What doſt thou want, thou ſtorm-beat' maid,
" That thou theſe portals paſt ?
" Ill ſuiteth here thy looks diſmay'd,
" Thou art no bidden gueſt.

O chide not ! ſaid a gentle page,
　And wip'd his tear-wet cheek,
" Who would not ſhun the winter's rage ?
　" The wind is cold and bleak.

" Her robe is ſtiff with drizly ſnow,
　" And rent her mantle grey ;
" None ever bade the wretched go
　" Upon his wedding-day."

　　　　Then

Then to his lord he hied him ſtraight,
   Where round on ſilken ſeat
Sat many a courteous dame and knight,
   And made obeiſance meet.

" There is a ſtranger in your hall,
   " Who wears no common mien ;
" Hard were the heart, as flinty wall,
   " That would not take her in.

" A fairer dame in hall or bower
   " Mine eyes did ne'er behold ;
" Tho' ſhelter'd in no father's tower,
   " And turn'd out to the cold.

" Her face is like an early morn,
   " Dimm'd with the nightly dew ;
" Her ſkin is like the ſheeted torn,
   " Her eyes are wat'ry blue.

                                    " And

" And tall and flender is her form,
    " Like willow o'er the brook ;
" But on her brow there broods a ftorm,
    " And reftlefs is her look,

" And well her troubled motions fhew
    " The tempeft in her mind ;
" Like the unfhelter'd fapling bough
    " Vex'd with the wintry wind.

" Her head droops on her ungirt breaft,
    " And fcatter'd is her hair ;
" Yet lady brac'd in courtly veft
    " Was never half fo fair.

Reverfe, and cold the turning blood
    The bridegroom's cheek forfook :
He fhook and ftagger'd as he ftood,
    And falter'd as he fpoke.

H 4   So

" So foft and fair I know a maid,

    " 'There is but only fhe;

" A wretched man her love betray'd,

    " And wretched let him be."

Deep frowning, turn'd the bride's dark eye,

    For bridal morn unmeet;

With trembling fteps her lord did hie

    The ftranger fair to greet.

Tho' loofe in fcatter'd weeds array'd,

    And ruffled with the ftorm;

Like lambkin from its fellows ftray'd,

    He knew her graceful form.

But when he fpy'd her funken eye,

    And features fharp and wan,

He heav'd a deep and heavy figh,

    And down the big tears ran.

                        " Why

" Why droops thy head, thou lovely maid,
    " Upon thy hand of fnow?
" Is it becaufe thy love betray'd,
    " That thou art brought fo low ?

Quick from her eye the keen glance came
    Who queftion'd her to fee :
And oft fhe mutter'd o'er his name,
    And wift not it was he.

Full hard againft his writhing brows
    His clenched hands he preft;
Full high his lab'ring bofom rofe,
    And rent its filken veft.

" O curfed be the golden price,
    " That did my bafenefs prove !
" And curfed be my friends advice,
    " That wil'd me from thy love !

                        " And

" And curſed be the woman's art,

 " That lur'd me to her ſnare!

" And curſed be the faithleſs heart

 " That left thee to deſpair!

" Yet now I'll hold thee to my ſide,

 " Tho' worthleſs I have been,

" Nor friends, nor wealth, nor dizen'd bride,

 " Shall ever ſtand between.

" When thou art weary and depreſs'd,

 " I'll lull thee to thy ſleep;

" And when dark fancies vex thy breaſt,

 " I'll ſit by thee and weep.

" I'll tend thee like a reſtleſs child

 " Where'er thy rovings be;

" Nor geſture keen, nor eye-ball wild,

 " Shall turn my love from thee.

       " Night

" Night ſhall not hang cold o'er thy head,

 " And I ſecurely lie ;

" Nor drizly clouds upon thee ſhed,

 " And I in covert dry.

" I'll ſhare the cold blaſt on the heath,

 " I'll ſhare thy wants and pain :

" Nor friend nor foe, nor life nor death,

 " Shall ever make us twain."

THUNDER.

THUNDER.

SPIRIT of strength, to whom in wrath 'tis given

To mar the earth, and shake the vasty heaven:

Behold the gloomy robes, that spreading hide

Thy secret majesty, lo! flow and wide,

Thy heavy skirts sail in the middle air,

Thy sultry shroud is o'er the noonday glare:

Th' advancing clouds sublimely roll'd on high,

Deep in their pitchy volumes clothe the sky:

Like hosts of gath'ring foes array'd in death,

Dread hangs their gloom upon the earth beneath.

It is thy hour: the awful deep is still,

And laid to rest the wind of ev'ry hill.

Wild creatures of the forest homeward scour,

And in their dens with fear unwonted cow'r.

Pride

Pride in the lordly palace is forgot,
And in the lowly ſhelter of the cot
The poor man ſits, with all his fam'ly round,
In awful expectation of thy ſound.
Lone on his way the trav'ller ſtands aghaſt;
The fearful looks of man to heav'n are caſt,
When, lo! thy lightning gleams on high,
As ſwiftly turns his ſtartled eye;
And ſwiftly as thy ſhooting blaze
Each half performed motion ſtays,
Deep awe, all human ſtrife and labour ſtills,
And thy dread voice alone, the earth and heaven fills.

Bright burſts the lightning from the cloud's dark
   womb,
As quickly ſwallow'd in the cloſing gloom.
The diſtant ſtreamy flaſhes, ſpread aſkance
In paler ſheetings, ſkirt the wide expanſe.
Dread flaming from aloft, the cat'ract dire
Oft meets in middle ſpace the nether fire.

Fierce,

Fierce, red, and ragged, ſhiv'ring in the air,
Athwart mid-darkneſs ſhoots the lengthen'd glare.
Wild glancing round, the feebler lightning plays;
The rifted centre pours the gen'ral blaze;
And from the warring clouds in fury driven *,
Red writhing falls the keen embodied bolt of heaven.

From the dark bowels of the burthen'd cloud
Dread ſwells the rolling peal, full, deep'ning, loud.
Wide ratt'ling claps the heavens ſcatter'd o'er,
In gather'd ſtrength lift the tremendous roar;
With weaning force it rumbles over head,
Then, growling, wears away to ſilence dread.
Now waking from afar in doubled might,
Slow rolling onward to the middle height;
Like craſh of mighty mountains downward hurl'd,
Like the upbreaking of a wrecking world,

* In poetry we have only to do with appearances; and the
zig-zag lightning, commonly thought to be the thunder-bolt, is
certainly firm and embodied, compared to the ordinary lightning,
which takes no diſtinct ſhape at all.

In

In dreadful majesty, th' explosion grand
Bursts wide, and awful, o'er the trembling land.
The lofty mountains echo back the roar,
Deep from afar rebounds earth's rocky shore;
All else existing in the senses bound
Is lost in the immensity of sound.
Wide jarring sounds by turns in strength convene,
And deep, and terrible, the solemn pause between.

Aloft upon the mountain's side
The kindled forest blazes wide.
Huge fragments of the rugged steep
Are tumbled to the lashing deep.
Firm rooted in the cloven rock,
Loud crashing falls the stubborn oak.
The lightning keen, in wasteful ire,
Fierce darting on the lofty spire,
Wide rends in twain the ir'n-knit stone,
And stately tow'rs are lowly thrown.

Wild

Wild flames o'erfcour the wide campaign,
And plough afkance the hiffing main.
Nor ftrength of man may brave the ftorm,
Nor fhelter fkreen the fhrinking form ;
Nor caftle wall its fury ftay,
Nor maffy gate may bar its way.
It vifits thofe of low eftate,
It fhakes the dwellings of the great,
It looks athwart the fecret tomb,
And glares upon the prifon's gloom ;
While dungeons deep, in unknown light,
Flafh hidious on the wretches' fight,
And lowly groans the downward cell,
Where deadly filence wont to dwell.

Now upcaft eyes to heav'n adore,
And knees that never bow'd before.
In ftupid wonder ftares the child ;
The maiden turns her glances wild,

And

And lifts to hear the coming roar :

The aged fhake their locks fo hoar :

And ftouteft hearts begin to fail,

And many a manly cheek is pale ;

Till nearer clofing peals aftound,

And crafhing ruin mingles round ;

Then 'numbing fear awhile up-binds

The paufing action of their minds,

Till wak'd to dreadful fenfe, they lift their eyes,

And round the ftricken corfe, fhrill fhrieks of horror

rife.

Now thinly fpreads the falling hail

A motly winter o'er the vale,

The hailftones bounding as they fall

On hardy rock, or ftorm-beat' wall.

The loud beginning peal its fury checks,

Now full, now fainter, with irreg'lar breaks,

Then weak in force, unites the fcatter'd found ;

And rolls its lengthen'd grumblings to the diftant bound.

I   A thick

A thick and muddy whitenefs clothes the fky,

In paler flafhes gleams the lightning by;

And thro' the rent cloud, filver'd with his ray,

The fun looks down on all this wild affray;

As high enthron'd above all mortal ken,

A greater Pow'r beholds the ftrife of men:

Yet o'er the diftant hills the darknefs fcowls,

And deep, and long, the parting tempeft growls.

WIND.

W I N D.

Pow'r uncontrollable, who hold'ſt thy ſway
In the unbounded air, whoſe trackleſs way
Is in the firmament, unknown of ſight,
Who bend'ſt the ſheeted heavens in thy might,
And lift'ſt the ocean from its loweſt bed
To join in middle ſpace the conflict dread;
Who o'er the peopled earth in ruin ſcours,
And buffets the firm rock that proudly low'rs,
Thy ſigns are in the heav'ns.   The upper clouds
Draw ſhapeleſs o'er the ſky their miſty ſhrowds;
Whilſt darker fragments rove in lower bands,
And mournful purple cloaths the diſtant lands.
In gather'd tribes, upon the hanging peak
The ſea-fowl ſcream, ill-omen'd creatures ſhriek:

Unwonted

Unwonted founds groan on the diftant wave,

And murmurs deep break from the downward cave.

Unlook'd-for gufts the quiet forefts fhake,

And fpeak thy coming—awful Pow'r, awake!

Like burft of mighty waters wakes the blaft,

In wide and boundlefs fweep: thro' regions vaft

The floods of air in loofen'd fury drive,

And meeting currents ftrong, and fiercely ftrive.

Firft wildly raving on the mountain's brow

'Tis heard afar, till o'er the plains below

With even rufhing force it bears along,

And gradual fwelling, louder, full, and ftrong,

Breaks wide in fcatter'd bellowing thro' the air.

Now is it hufh'd to calm, now rous'd to war,

Whilft in the paufes of the nearer blaft,

The farther gufts howl from the diftant wafte.

Now rufhing furious by with loofen'd fweep,

Now rolling grandly on, folemn and deep,

In

Its burfting ftrength the full embodied found

In wide and fhallow brawlings fcatters round;

Then wild in eddies fhrill, with rage diftraught,

And force exhaufted, whiftles into naught.

With growing might, arifing in its room,

From far, like waves of ocean onward come

Succeeding gufts, and fpend their wafteful ire,

Then flow, in grumbled mutterings retire:

And folemn ftillnefs overawes the land,

Save where the tempeft growls along the diftant
    ftrand.

But great in doubled ftrength, afar and wide,

Returning battle wakes on ev'ry fide;

And rolling on with full and threat'ning found,

In wildly mingled fury clofes round.

With bellowings loud, and hollow deep'ning fwell,

Reiterated hifs, and whiftlings fhrill,

Fierce wars the varied ftorm, with fury tore,

Till all is overwhelm'd in one tremendous roar.

The vexed foreſt, toſſing wide,

Uprooted ſtrews its faireſt pride;

The lofty pine in twain is broke,

And cruſhing falls the knotted oak.

The huge rock trembles in its might;

The proud tow'r tumbles from its height;

Uncover'd ſtands the ſocial home;

High rocks aloft the city dome;

Whilſt burſting bar, and flapping gate,

And craſhing roof, and clatt'ring grate,

And hurling wall, and falling ſpire,

Mingle in jarring din and ruin dire.

Wild ruin ſcours the works of men;

Their motly fragments ſtrew the plain.

E'en in the deſert's pathleſs waſte,

Uncouth deſtruction marks the blaſt:

And hollow caves whoſe ſecret pride,

Groteſque and grand, was never ey'd

By mortal man, abide its drift,

Of many a goodly pillar reft.

Fierce

Fierce whirling mounts the defert fand,

And threats aloft the peopl'd land.

The great expanded ocean, heaving wide,

Rolls to the fartheft bound its lafhing tide;

Whilft in the middle deep afar are feen,

All ftately from the funken gulfs between,

The tow'ring waves, which bend with hoary
   brow,

Then dafh impetuous to the deep below.

With broader fweepy bafe, in gather'd might

Majeftic, fwelling to ftupendous height,

The mountain billow lifts its awful head,

And, curving, breaks aloft with roarings dread.

Sublimer ftill the mighty waters rife,

And mingle in the ftrife of nether fkies.

All wildnefs and uproar, above, beneath,

A world immenfe of danger, dread, and death.

  In dumb defpair the failor ftands,

The frantic merchant wrings his hands,

Advent'rous

Advent'rous hope clings to the yard,

And finking wretches fhriek unheard :

Whilft on the land, the matron ill at reft,

Thinks of the diftant main, and heaves her heavy breaft.

The peafants leave their ruin'd home,

And o'er the fields diftracted roam :

Infenfible the 'numbed infant fleeps,

And helplefs bending age, weak and unfhelter'd weeps.

Low fhrinking fear, in place of ftate,

Skulks in the dwellings of the great.

The rich man marks with careful eye,

Each wafteful guft that whiftles by ;

And ill men fcar'd with fancied fcreams

Sit lift'ning to the creaking beams.

At break of ev'ry rifing fquall

On ftorm-beat' roof, or ancient wall,

Full many a glance of fearful eye

Is upward caft, till from on high,

From cracking joift, and gaping rent,

And falling fragments warning fent,

                                        Loud

Loud wakes around the wild affray,
'Tis all confusion and difmay.

Now powerful but inconftant in its courfe,
The tempeft varies with uncertain force.
Like doleful wailings on the lonely wafte,
Solemn and dreary founds the weaning blaft.
Exhaufted gufts recoiling growl away,
And, wak'd anew, return with feebler fway;
Save where between the ridgy mountains pent,
The fierce imprifon'd current ftrives for vent,
With hollow howl, and lamentation deep,
Then rufhes o'er the plain with partial fweep.
A parting guft o'erfcours the weary land,
And lowly growls along the diftant ftrand :
Light thro' the wood the fhiv'ring branches play,
And on the ocean far it flowly dies away.

AN

AN ADDRESS TO THE NIGHT.

A FEARFUL MIND.

UNCERTAIN, awful as the gloom of death,
The Night's grim shadows cover all beneath.
Shapeless and black is ev'ry object round,
And lost in thicker gloom the distant bound.
Each swelling height is clad with dimmer shades,
And deeper darkness marks the hollow glades.
The moon in heavy clouds her glory veils,
And slow along their passing darkness sails;
While lesser clouds in parted fragments roam,
And red stars glimmer thro' the river's gloom.

Nor cheerful voice is heard from man's abode,
Nor sounding footsteps on the neighb'ring road;

Nor

Nor glimm'ring fire the diftant cottage tells;

On all around a fearful ftillnefs dwells:

The mingled noife of induftry is laid,

And filence deepens with the nightly fhade.

Though ftill the haunts of men, and fhut their
    light,

Thou art not filent, dark myfterious Night.

The cries of favage creatures wildly break

Upon thy quiet; birds ill-omen'd fhrick;

Commotions ftrange difturb the ruftling trees;

And heavy plaints come on the paffing breeze.

Far on the lonely wafte, and diftant way,

Unwonted founds are heard, unknown of day.

With fhrilly fcreams the haunted cavern rings;

And heavy treading of unearthly things

Sounds loud and hollow thro' the ruin'd dome;

Yea, voices iffue from the fecret tomb.

  But lo! a fudden flow of burfting light!

What wild furrounding fcenes break on the fight!

Huge

Huge rugged rocks uncouthly low'r on high,
Whilſt on the plain their lengthen'd ſhadows lie.
The wooded banks in ſtreamy brightneſs glow ;
And waving darkneſs ſkirts the flood below.
The roving ſhadow haſtens o'er the ſtream ;
And like a ghoſt's pale ſhrowd the waters gleam.
Black fleeting ſhapes acroſs the valley ſtray :
Gigantic forms tow'r on the diſtant way :
The ſudden winds in wheeling eddies change :
'Tis all confus'd, unnatural, and ſtrange.
Now all again in horrid gloom is loſt :
Wild wakes the breeze like ſound of diſtant hoſt :
Bright ſhoots along the ſwift returning light :
Succeeding ſhadows cloſe the ſtartled ſight.
Some reſtleſs ſpirit holds the nightly ſway :
Long is the wild, and doubtful is my way.
Inconſtant Night, whate'er thy changes be,
It ſuits not man to be alone with thee.
O ! for the ſhelt'ring roof of loweſt kind,
Secure to reſt with others of my hind !

AN

AN ADDRESS TO THE NIGHT.

A DISCONTENTED MIND.

How thick the clouds of night are rang'd o'er
   head!
Confounding darkneſs o'er the earth is ſpread.
The clouded moon her cheering count'nance hides;
And feeble ſtars, between the ragged ſides
Of broken clouds, with unavailing rav,
Look thro' to mock the trav'ller on his way.
Tree, buſh, and rugged rock, and hollow dell,
In deeper ſhades their forms confus'dly tell,
To cheat the weary wand'rer's doubtful eye;
Whilſt chilly paſſing winds come ruffling by;

And

And tangled briars perplex the darken'd paſs;
And ſlimy reptiles glimmer on the graſs;
And ſtinging night-flies ſpend their curſed ſpite;
Unhoſpitable are thy ſhades, O Night!

Now hard ſuſpicion bars the creaking door;
And ſafe within the ſelfiſh worldlings ſnore:
And wealthy fools are warm in downy bed:
And houſeleſs beggars ſhelter in the ſhed:
And neſtling coveys cow'r beneath the brake;
While prowling miſchief only is awake.
Each hole and den ſends forth its curſed brood,
And ſavage bloody creatures range the wood.
The thieviſh vagrant plies his thriftleſs trade
Beneath the friendly ſhelter of the ſhade;
Whilſt boldeſt riſk the lawleſs robber braves:
The day for fools was made, and night for knaves.

O welcome,

O welcome, kindly moon ! thy light diſplay,

And guide a weary trav'ller on his way.

Hill, wood, and valley, brighten in her beam ;

And wavy ſilver glitters on the ſtream.

The diſtant path-way ſhews diſtinct and clear,

From far inviting, but perplex'd when near.

For blackning ſhadows add deceitful length,

And leſſer objects gain unwonted ſtrength ;

Each ſtep miſguiding; to the eye unknown,

The ſhining gutter, from the gliſt'ning ſtone ;

While croſſing ſhadows checker o'er the ground,

The more perplexing for the brightneſs round.

Deceitful are thy ſmiles, untoward Night !

Thy gloom is better than miſguiding light.

Then welcome is yon cloud that onward ſails,

And all this glary ſhew in darkneſs veils.

But ſee how ſoon the fleeting ſhade is paſt,

And ſtreamy brightneſs ſhoots acroſs the waſte.

Now fly the ſhadows borne upon the wind ;

Succeeding brightneſs travels faſt behind.

And

And now it low'rs again.   Inconſtant Night,

Confound thy freaks ! be either dark or light.

Yet let them come ; whate'er thy changes be,

I was a fool to put my truſt in thee.

AN

AN ADDRESS TO THE NIGHT.

A SORROWFUL MIND.

How lone and dreary hangs the fombre Night
O'er wood and valley, ftream and craggy height!
While nearer objects, bufh, and waving bough,
Their dark uncertain forms but dimly fhow;
Like thofe with which difturbed fancies teem,
And fhape the fcen'ry of a gloomy dream.
The moon is cover'd with her fable fhrowd;
And o'er the heav'ns rove many a dufky cloud;
Thro' ragged rents the paly fky is feen,
And feebly glance the twinkling ftars between:
Whilft earth below is wrapt in ftilly gloom,
All fad and filent as the clofed tomb.

K   No

No bleating flock is heard upon the vale;

Nor lowing kine upon the open dale;

Nor voice of hunter on the lonely heath;

Nor found of trav'ller on the diftant path.

Shut is the fenced door of man's abode;

And ruffling breezes only are abroad.

How mournful is thy voice, O nightly gale!

Acrofs the wood, or down the narrow vale;

And fad, tho' fecret and unknown they be,

The fighs of woeful hearts that wake with thee.

For now no friends the haunts of forrow feek;

Tears hang unchidden on the mourner's cheek:

No fide-look vexes from the curious eye;

Nor calm reproving reafoner is by:

The kindly cumbrous vifitor is gone,

And laden fpirits love to figh alone.

O Night! wild fings the wind, deep low'rs the
  fhade;

Thy robe is gloomy, and thy voice is fad:

But

But weary souls confin'd in earthly cell
Are deep in kindred gloom, and love thee well.

But now the veiling darkness passes by;
The moon unclouded holds the middle sky.
A soft and mellow light is o'er the wood;
And silv'ry pureness sparkles on the flood.
White tow'r the clifts from many a craggy breach;
The brown heath shews afar its dreary stretch.
While fairer as the brighten'd object swells,
Fast by its side the darker shadow dwells:
The lofty mountains form the deeper glade,
And keener light but marks the blacker shade.
Then welcome yonder clouds that swiftly sail,
And o'er yon glary op'ning draw the veil.
But, ah! too swiftly flies the friendly shade!
Returning brightness travels up the glade,
And all is light again. O fickle Night!
No traveller is here to bless thy light.

I seek

I feek nor home, nor fhed ; I have no way ;

Why fend thy beams to one who cannot ftray ?

Or wood, or defert, is the fame to me ;

O low'r again, and let me reft with thee !

AN

AN ADDRESS TO THE NIGHT.

A JOYFUL MIND,

THE warping gloom of night is gather'd round;
And varied darkness marks the uneven ground.
A dimmer shade is on the mountain's brow,
And deeper low'rs the lengthen'd vale below;
While nearer objects all enlarg'd and dark,
Their strange and shapeless forms uncouthly mark;
Which thro' muddy night are dimly shown,
Like old companions in a garb unknown.
The heavy sheeted clouds are spread on high,
And streaky darkness bounds the farther sky:
And swift along the lighter vagrants sweep,
Whilst clear stars thro' their riven edges peep.

Soft

Soft thro' each ragged breach, and ſtreamy rent,

And open gaps in duſky circle pent,

The upper heaven looks ſerenely bright

In dappled gold, and ſnowy fleeces dight:

And on the middle current lightly glides

The leſſer cloud, with ſilver wreathy ſides.

In ſudden guſts awakes the nightly breeze

Acroſs the wood, and ruſtles thro' the trees;

Or whiſtles on the plain with eddying ſweep;

Or iſſues from the glen in wailings deep,

Which die away upon the open vale:

Whilſt in the pauſes of the ruffling gale

The buzzing night-fly riſes from the ground,

And wings his flight in many a mazy round;

And lonely owls begin their nightly ſtrain,

So hateful to the ear of 'nighted ſwain.

Thou do'ſt the weary trav'ller miſlead;

Thy voice is roughſome, and uncooth thy weed,

O gloomy Night! for black thy ſhadows be,

And fools have rais'd a bad report on thee.

Yet

Yet art thou free and friendly to the gay,

And light hearts prize thee equal to the day.

Now tirefome plodding folks are gone to reſt;

And foothing ſlumber locks the careful breaſt.

And tell-tale friends, and wife advifers fnore;

And foftly ſlip-ſhod youths unbar the door.

Now footſteps echo far, and watch-dogs bark;

Worms glow, and cats' eyes glitter in the dark.

The vagrant lover croſſes moor and hill,

And near the lowly cottage whiſtles ſhrill:

Or, bolder grown, beneath the friendly ſhade,

Taps at the window of his fav'rite maid;

Who from above his fimple tale receives,

Whilſt ſtupid matrons ſtart, and think of thieves.

Now daily fools unbar the narrow foul,

All wife and gen'rous o'er the nightly bowl.

The haunted wood receives its motley hoſt,

(By trav'ller ſhun'd) tho' neither fag nor ghoſt;

And

And there the crackling bonfire blazes red,

While merry vagrants feaſt beneath the ſhed.

From ſleepleſs beds unquiet ſpirits riſe,

And cunning wags put on their borrow'd guiſe:

Whilſt ſilly maidens mutter o'er their boon,

And crop their fairy weeds beneath the moon:

And harmleſs plotters ſlyly take the road,

And trick and playful miſchief is abroad.

But, lo! the moon looks forth in ſplendour bright,

Fair and unclouded, from her middle height.

The paſſing cloud unveils her kindly ray,

And ſlowly ſails its weary length away:

While broken fragments from its fleecy ſide,

In duſky bands before it ſwiftly glide;

Their miſty texture changing with the wind,

A ſtrange and ſcatter'd group, of motley kind

As ever earth or fruitful ocean fed,

Or ever youthful poets fancy bred.

His

His furgy length the wreathing ferpent trails,

And by his fide the rugged camel fails:

The winged griffith follows clofe behind,

And fpreads his dufky pinions to the wind.

Athwart the fky in fcatter'd bands they range

From fhape to fhape, transform'd in endlefs change;

Then piece meal torn, in ragged portions ftray,

Or thinly fpreading, flowly melt away.

A fofter brightnefs covers all below;

Hill, dale, and wood, in mellow'd colour's glow.

High tow'rs the whiten'd rock in added ftrength;

The brown heath fhews afar its dreary length.

The winding river glitters on the vale;

And gilded trees wave in the paffing gale.

Upon the ground each black'ning fhadow lies,

And hafty darknefs o'er the valley flies.

Wide fheeting fhadows travel o'er the plain,

And fwiftly clofe upon the varied fcene.

Return, O lovely moon! and look from high,

All ftately riding in thy motled fky.

Yet,

Yet, O thy beams in hafty vifits come !

As fwiftly follow'd by the fleeting gloom.

O Night ! thy fmiles are fhort, and fhort thy fhade ;

Thou art a freakifh friend, and all unftay'd :

Yet from thy varied changes who are free ?

Full many an honeft friend refembles thee.

Then let my doubtful footfteps darkling ftray,

Thy next fair beam will fet me on my way :

E'en take thy freedom, whether rough or kind,

I came not forth to quarrel with the wind.

TO

TO FEAR.

O THOU! before whose haggard eyes
A thousand images arise,
Whose forms of horror none may see,
But with a soul disturb'd by thee!
Wilt thou for ever haunt mankind,
And glare upon the darken'd mind!
Whene'er thou enterest a breast,
Thou robb'st it of its joy and rest;
And terrible, and strange to tell,
On what that mind delights to dwell.
The ruffian's knife with reeking blade,
The stranger murder'd in his bed:
The howling wind, the raging deep,
The sailor's cries, the sinking ship:

The

The awful thunder breaking round :

The yauning gulf, the rocking ground :

The precipice, whofe low'ring brow

O'erhangs the horrid deep below ;

And tempts the wretch, worn out with ftrife,

Of worldly cares, to end his life.

But when thou raifeft to the fight

Unearthly forms that walk the night,

The chilly blood, with magic art,

Runs backward on the ftouteft heart.

Lo ! in his poft the foldier ftands * !

The deadly weapon in his hands.

In front of death he rufhes on,

Renown with life is cheaply won,

Whilft all his foul with ardour burns,

And to the thickeft danger turns.

But fee the man alone, unbent,

A church-yard near, and twilight fpent,

* See Spectator, No. 12.

Returning

Returning late to his abode,

Upon an unfrequented road:

No choice is left, his feet muſt tread

The awful dwelling of the dead.

In foul miſt doth the pale moon wade,

No twinkling ſtar breaks thro' the ſhade:

Thick rows of trees increaſe the gloom,

And awful ſilence of the tomb.

Swift to his thoughts, unbidden, throng

Full many a tale, forgotten long,

Of ghoſts, who at the dead of night

Walk round their graves all wrapt in white,

And o'er the church-yard dark and drear,

Becken the traveller to draw near:

And reſtleſs ſprites, who from the ground,

Juſt as the midnight clock doth ſound,

Riſe ſlowly to a dreadful height,

Then vaniſh quickly from the ſight:

And wretches who, returning home,

By chance have ſtumbled near ſome tomb,

Athwart

Athwart a coffin or a bone,

And three times heard a hollow groan;

With fearful steps he takes his way,

And shrinks, and wishes it were day.

He starts and quakes at his own tread,

But dare not turn about his head.

Some found he hears on ev'ry side;

And thro' the trees strange phantoms glide.

His heart beats thick against his breast,

And hardly stays within its chest:

Wild and unsettled are his eyes;

His quicken'd hairs begin to rise:

Ghastly and strong his features grow;

The cold dew trickles from his brow;

Whilst grinning beat his clatt'ring teeth,

And loosen'd knock his joints beneath.

As to the charnel he draws nigh

The whiten'd tomb-stone strikes his eye:

He starts, he stops, his eye-balls glare,

And settle in a death-like stare:

Deep

Deep hollow founds ring in his ear;
Such founds as dying wretches hear
When the grim dreaded tyrant calls,
A horrid found, he groans and falls.

Thou do'ft our faireft hope deftroy;
Thou art a gloom o'er ev'ry joy;
Unheeded let my dwelling be,
O Fear! but far remov'd from thee!

A STORY

A STORY OF OTHER TIMES.

SOMEWHAT IN IMITATION OF THE POEMS OF
OSSIAN.

LATHMOR.

BUT why do'st thou stop on the way, and hold
    me thus hard in thy grasp?

It was but the voice of the winds from the deep
    narrow glens of Glanarven.

ALLEN.

The heath is unruffled around, and the oak o'er
    thy head is at rest:

Calm swells the moon on the lake, and nothing is
    heard in the reeds.

Sad

Sad was the found, O my father ! but it was not the
  voice of the wind.

LATHMOR.

What dark tow'ring rock do I fee 'midft the grey
  fpreading mift of the hills ?

This is not the vale of Clanarven : my fon, we have
  err'd from the way.

ALLEN.

It is not a dark tow'ring rock, 'midft the grey
  fettled mift of the hills.

'Tis a dark tow'r of ftrength which thou feeft, and
  the ocean fpreads dimly behind it.

LATHMOR.

Then here will we ftop for the night, for the
  tow'r of Arthula is near.

Proceed not, my fon, on the way, for it was not the
  voice of the wind.

L   The

The ghoſt of the valliant is forth; and it mourns round the place of its woe.

The trav'ller oft' hears it at midnight, and turns him aſide from its haunt.

The ſharp moon is ſpent in her courſe, and the way of the deſert is doubtful.

This oak with his wide leavy branches will ſhelter our heads from the night;

And I'll tell thee a ſtory of old, ſince the tow'r of Arthula is near.

From the walls of his ſtrength came Lochallen, with his broad cheſted ſons of the hills.

He was ſtrong as a bull of the foreſt, and keen as a bird of the rock.

His friends of the chace were around him, the ſons of the heroes of Mora.

They were clad in the ſtrength of their youth; and the ſound of their arms rung afar.

For

For Uthal had led his dark hoft from the blue mifty
    ifle of his power;

And o'erfpread like a cloud of the defert, the land of
    the white-headed Lorma.

Of Lorma who fat in the hall, and lamented the fons
    of his youth;

For Orvina remained alone to fupport the frail fteps of
    his age.

He fent to the king of Ithona: he remembered the
    love of his father:

And Lochallen foon join'd him on Loarn with the
    high minded chieftains of Mora.

Loud was the found of the battle, and many the flain
    of the field.

Red was the fword of Lochallen: it was red with the
    blood of the brave.

For his eye fought the combat of heroes, and the
    mighty withftood not his arm.

L 2

He

He rag'd like a flame on the heath; and the enemy
fled from his face.

But fhort was the triumph of Lorma; the hour of his
fading was near.

Whilft a bard rais'd the fong of the battle, his dim
eyes were clofed in death.

He fell like a ruined tow'r; like a fragment of times
that are paft:

Like a rock whofe foundation is worn with the lafhes
of many a wave.

Four grey head warriors of Lorma remain'd from the
days of his youth:

They mourn'd o'er the fall of their lord; and they bore
him to his dark narrow houfe.

His memorial was rais'd on the hill; and the lovely
Orvina wept over it.

She bent her fair form o'er the heap; and her forrow
was filent, and gentle.

It

It flow'd like the pure twinkling ſtream beneath the
    green ſhade of the fern.

The hunters oft bleſs it at noon, tho' the ſtrangers
    perceive not its courſe.

The wind of the hill rais'd her locks, and Lochallen
    beheld her in grief.

The ſoul of the hero was knit to the tear-eyed daugh-
    ter of Lorma.

She was graceful and tall as the willow, that bends
    o'er the deep ſhady ſtream.

Her eye like a ſun-beam on water, that gleams thro'
    the dark ſkirting reeds.

Her hair like the light wreathing cloud, that floats on
    the brow of the hill,

When the beam of the morning is there, and it ſcat-
    ters its ſkirts to the wind.

Lovely and ſoft were her ſmiles, like a glimpſe from
    the white riven cloud,

When the ſun haſtens over the lake, and a ſummer
    ſhow'r ruffles its boſom.

                Her

Her voice was the fweet found of midnight, that vi-
fits the ear of the bard,

When he ftarts from the place of his flumber, and
calls on fome far diftant friend.

She was fair 'mongft the maids of her time; and fhe
foften'd the wrath of the mighty.

Their eyes lighten'd up in her prefence; they dropt
their dark fpears as fhe fpoke.

Lochallen was firm in his ftrength, and unmov'd in
the battle of heroes;

Like a rock-fenced ifle of the ocean, that fhews its
dark head thro' the ftorm.

His brow was like a cliff on the fhore, that fore-
warneth the hunters of Ithona;

For there gleams the firft ray of morning, and there
broods the mift ere the ftorm:

It fhone, and it darken'd by turns, as the ftrength of
his paffions arofe.

He was terrible as a gathering ftorm, when his foul
learnt the wrongs of the feeble.

His

His eye was the lightning of fhields; he was fwift as
a blaft in its courfe.

When the warriours return'd from the field, and the
fons of the mighty affembled,

He was graceful as the light tow'ring cloud that rifes
from the blue bounded main.

Gentle and fair was his form in the tow'rs of the hilly
Ithona.

His voice cheer'd the foul of the fad; he would fport
with a child in the hall.

Matchlefs in the days of their love were Lochallen
and the daughter of Lorma.

But their beauty has ceas'd on Arthula; and the place
of their reft is unknown.

The family of Lorma has fail'd, and ftrangers rejoice
in his hall:

But voices of forrow are heard when the ftillnefs of
midnight is there;

The

The ſtranger is wak'd with the ſound, and enquires of
the race that is gone.

But wherefore thus doleful and ſad, do ye wander alone
on Arthula?

Why look ye thus lonely and ſad, ye children of the
dark narrow houſe?

Your names ſhall be known in the ſong, when the
fame of the mighty is low.

ALLEN.

From what cloud of the hills do they look? for I ſee
not their forms, O my father!

LATHMOR.

Why do'ſt thou tremble my ſon? thou haſt fought in
the battle of ſhields.

They look'd from no cloud of the hills; but the ſoul
of thy father beheld them.

Lochallen

Lochallen return'd from the field, to the fea-beaten
    tower of Arthula.

Five days he abode in the hall, and they pafs'd like a
    glimpfe of the fun,

When the clouds of the tempeft are rent, and the
    green ifland fmiles 'midft the ftorm.

On the fixth a cloud hung on his brow, and his eye
    fhun'd the looks of his friends.

He fpoke to the maid of his foul, and the trouble of
    his bofom was great.

Pleafant is the hall of my love; but the ftorm gathers
    round us, Orvina.

I muft go to the ifland of Uthal, and fcatter his ga-
    thering force.

But like a cleft oak of the foreft, I'll quickly return
    to my love:

When the hard wedge is drawn from its fide, it returns
    to itfelf again.

The daughter of Lorma was filent: fhe turn'd her
    fair face from his fight.

Go

Go to the war, fon of Mora; and the ftrength of thy
    fathers go with thee.

I will fit on the high rocky fhore, and look o'er the
    wide foaming fea.

I will watch ev'ry blue rifing cloud, till I fee thy dark
    veffels return.

He gather'd his warriours around him; they darken'd
    the brown rugged fhore.

The rocks echo'd wide to their cries, and loud was
    the dafhing of oars.

Orvina ftood high on a rock, that hung o'er the deep
    lafhing main;

Big fwell'd the tear in her eye, and high heav'd the
    fighs of her bofom;

As fhe faw the white billows encreafing between his
    dark fhip and the fhore.

Her fixed eye follow'd its courfe o'er many a far dif-
    tant wave,

Till

Till its broad fails, and high tow'ring maft but ap-
    pear'd like a fpeck on the waters;

Yet ftill fhe beheld in her fancy the form of her love
    on its fide;

And fhe ftretched her white arms to the ocean, and
    wav'd her loofe girdle on high.

Soon reach'd the fons of Ithona the blue mifty ifle
    of their foe.

Like the pent up dogs of the hunter when let loofe
    from their prifon of night;

Who fnuff up the air of the morning, and rejoice at
    the voice of the chace;

They leapt from the fides of their veffels, and fpread
    o'er the wiae foundıng fhore.

Thick on the brown heathy plain, were fpread the
    dark thoufands of Uthal.

The warriours of Lochallen were few, but their fa
    thers were known in the fong.

                    Like

Like a small rapid stream of the hills when it falls on
the broad settled lake,

And troubles its dark muddy bosom, and dashes its
waters aloft,

So rush'd the keen sons of Ithona on the thick ga-
ther'd host of the foe.

Red gleam'd the arms of the brave thro' the brown
rising dust of the field.

Fierce glar'd the eyes of Lochallen; he sought the
dark face of his enemy.

He found the grim king of the isle; but the strength
of his chieftains was round him.

Come forth in thy might, said Lochallen; come forth
to the combat of kings.

Great is the might of thy warriours; but where is the
strength of thine arms?

Youth of Ithona, said Uthal, thy fathers were mighty
in battle,

Return to thy brown woody hills, till the hair is grown
dark on thy cheek;

Then

Then come from the tow'rs of thy safety, a foe less
unworthy of Uthal.

But thou lovest a weakly enemy, foe of the white
haired chief.

Thou lovest a foe that is weak, said the red swelling
pride of Lochallen.

Seest thou this sword of my youth? it is red with the
blood of thy heroes.

Come forth in the strength of thine years, and hand
its dark blade in thy hall.

He lifted a spear in his wrath o'er the head of his high
worded foe;

But the strength of his chieftains was there, and it rung
on their broad spreading shields.

He turned himself scornful away, to look for some
nobler enemy;

He met thee fair son of Hidallo, as chaffing he strode
in his wrath;

But thou never did'st turn from the valiant, youth
of the far distant land.

Fierce

Fierce fought the heroes, and wonder'd each chief at the might of his foe.

They found themfelves matched in ftrength, and they fought in the pride of their fouls.

Bloody and long was the fight, but the arm of Loch-allen prevail'd.

Ah, why did you combat, ye heroes! ah, why did ye meet in the field!

Your fouls had been brothers of love, had ye met in the dwellings of peace.

He was like to thyfelf, fon of Mora, where his voice cheer'd the heart of the ftranger

In the far diftant hall of his father, who never fhall hear it again;

He was like to thyfelf whom thou fleweft; and he fell in his youth like thee.

The maid of thy bofom is lovely, thou fair fallen fon of the ftranger.

She fits on her high hanging bower, and looks to the way of thy promife.

She

She combs down her long yellow hair; and prepares
a fine robe for thy coming.

She ſtarts at the voice of the breeze, and runs to the
door of her bow'r.

But thou art a dim miſty form on the clouds of far
diſtant hills.

Fierce was the rage of the battle, and terrible the
clanging of arms.

Loud were the ſhouts of the mighty, like the wide
ſcatter'd thunder of Lora,

When its voice is return'd from the rocks, and it
ſtrengthens in its broad ſpreading courſe.

Heavy were the groans of the dying; the voice of the
fallen was ſad,

Like the deep 'priſon'd winds of the cavern, when the
roar of the tempeſt is laid.

The ſons of Ithona were terrible: the enemy fled from
before them,

Like

Like the dark gather'd fowls of the ocean, that flock
to the fhore ere a ftorm.

They fled from the might of their foes, and the dark-
nefs of night clos'd around them.

Cold rofe the wind of the defert, and blew o'er the
dark bloody field.

Sad was its voice on the heath, where it lifted the locks
of the dead.

Hollow roar'd the fea at a diftance : the ghofts of the
flain fhriek'd aloud.

Pale fhady forms ftalk'd around, and their airy fwords
gleam'd thro' the night ;

For the fpirits of warriours departed came born on the
deep rufhing blaft ;

There hail'd they their new fallen fons, and the found
of their meeting was terrible.

At a diftance was gather'd Ithona round many a bright
flaming oak ;

'Till

Till morning rofe red o'er the main, like a new
  bloody field of battle.

Lochallen affembled his heroes; they rang'd o'er the
  land of their enemy.

But they found not the king in the field; and the
  walls of his ftrength were deferted.

Then fpoke the friend of his bofom, the dark haired
  chief of Trevallen;

Why feek you the king in his tow'rs? he is fled to
  the caves of his fear.

Let us fly, faid the chief of Ithona, let us fly to the
  daughter of Lorma!

Let us fight with man in the field, but pull not a
  deer from his den.

Two days they buried their dead, and rais'd their
  memorial on high.

On the third day they loofen'd their veffels, and left
  the blue ifle of their fame.

M

The

The darknefs of night was around when the bay of
Arthula receiv'd them.

Thick beat the joy of his bofom, as he drew near
the place of his love;

But the ftrength of his limbs was unloos'd, as he trode
on the dark founding fhore.

Thou did'ft promife, O maid of my foul! thou did'ft
promife to watch for thy love!

But no kindly meffenger waits to hail my return
from the war.

The tow'r of Arthula is dark; and I hear not the
found of its hall.

The watch dog howls to the night, nor heeds the ap-
proach of our feet.

He feized a bright flaming brand, and he haften'd
his fteps to the tow'r.

Wide ftood the black low'ring gate; and deep was
the filence within.

Hollow and loud rung his fteps, as he trode thro' the
dark empty hall.

He

He flew to the bow'r of his love ; it was ſtill as the
chamber of death.

His eyes ſearch'd wildly around him ; he call'd on
the name of his love ;

But his own voice returned alone from the deep-
ſounding walls of the tow'r.

He leant with his back to the wall, and croſs'd his
arms over his breaſt.

Heavy ſunk his head on his ſhoulder : the blue flame
burnt double before him.

A voice, like the evening breeze when it ſteals down
the bed of the river,

Came ſoftly and ſad to his ear, and he raiſed his
drooping head.

The form of his love ſtood before him : yet it was
not the form of his love ;

For fixed and dim was her eye, and the beams of her
beauty were fled.

She was pale as the white frozen lake, when it gleams
to the light of the moon.

Her

Her garments were heavy and drench'd, and the
  ftreams trickled faft from her hair.

She was like a fnow-crufted tree in winter, when it
  drops to the mid-day fun.

O feek not for me, fon of Moro, in the light cheer-
  ful dwellings of men!

For low is my bed in the deep, and cold is the place
  of my reft.

The fea monfter fports by my fide, and the water-
  fnake twines round my neck.

But do not forget me, Lochallen: O think on the
  days of our love!

I fat on the high rocky fhore, mine eyes look'd afar
  o'er the ocean.

I faw two dark fhips on the waves, and quick beat
  the joy of my breaft.

One veffel drew near to the fhore, and fix warriours
  leapt from its fide.

I haften'd to meet thee, my love; but mine ear met
  the ftern voice of Uthal.

I thought

I thought that my hero was flain, and I felt me alone in my weaknefs.

I felt me deferted and lonely: I flew to the fteep hanging rock:

I threw my robe over my head; and I hid me in the dark clofing deep.

Yet O do not leave me, Lochallen, to wafte in my watery bed!

But raife me a tomb on the hill, where the daughter of Lorma fhould lie.

The voice of her forrow did ceafe; and her form paffed quickly away.

It pafs'd like the pale fhiv'ring light, that is loft in the dark clofing cloud.

But, lo! the firft light of the morning is red on the fkirts of the heavens.

Let us go on my journey, my fon, for the length of the heath is before us.

M 3   ALLEN.

ALLEN.

It is not the light of the morn which thou fee'ft on the fkirts of the heavens;

It is but a clear fhiv'ring brightnefs, that changes its hue to the night.

I have feen it like a bloody-fpread robe when it hung o'er the waves of the North.

Sad was the fate of his love, but how fell the king of Ithona?

I have heard of the ftrength of his arm; did he fall in the battle of heroes?

LATHMOR.

He fell in the ftrength of his youth, but he fell not in battle, my fon.

He knew not the fword of a foe, yet he died not the death of the peaceful.

They carried them both to the hill, but the place of their reft is unknown.

ALLEN.

ALLEN.

But feeble and spent is thy voice, thou grey haired
bard of the hill.

LATHMOR.

Long is this song of the night, and I feel not the
strength of my youth.

ALLEN.

Then let us go on our way : let us go by the way of
the heath.

For it is the fair light of the morning which thou
see'st on the far bounding waves.

Slowly it grows in its beauty, and promises good to
the traveller.

Red are the small broken clouds that hang on the
skirts of the heavens.

Deep glows the clear open sky with the light of the
yet hidden sun,

M 4   Save

Save where the dark narrow cloud hath ſtretched its
    vaſt length o'er the heavens;

And the clear ruddy brightneſs behind it looks fair
    thro' its blue ſtreaming lines.

A bloom like the far diſtant heath is dark on the wide
    roving clouds.

The broad wavy breaſt of the ocean is grand in the
    beauty of morning.

Thick reſts the white ſettled miſt on the deep rugged
    clifts of the ſhore;

And the grey rocks look dimly between, like the high
    diſtant iſles in a calm.

But grim low'r the walks of Arthula; the light of the
    morn is behind them.

LATHMOR.

Dark low'rs the tow'r of Arthula: the time of its
    glory is paſt.

                           The

The valiant have ceas'd from its hall; and the fon of the ftranger is there.

The works of the mighty remain, but they are the vapour of morning.

A MOTHER

A MOTHER TO HER WAKING INFANT.

NOW in thy dazzling half-op'd eye,
Thy curled nofe, and lip awry,
Thy up-hoift arms, and noddling head,
And little chin with cryftal fpread,
Poor helplefs thing! what do I fee,
  That I fhould fing of thee?

From thy poor tongue no accents come,
Which can but rub thy toothlefs gum:
Small underftanding boaft thy face,
Thy fhapelefs limbs nor ftep, nor grace:

A few

A few ſhort words thy feats may tell,
  And yet I love thee well.

When ſudden wakes the bitter ſhriek,
And redder ſwells thy little cheek;
When rattled keys thy woe beguile,
And thro' the wet eye gleams the ſmile,
Still for thy weakly ſelf is ſpent
  Thy little ſilly plaint.

But when thy friends are in diſtreſs,
Thou'lt laugh and chuckle ne'er the leſs;
Nor e'en with ſympathy be ſmitten,
Tho' all are ſad but thee and kitten;
Yet little varlet that thou art,
  Thou twitcheſt at the heart.

Thy roſy cheek ſo ſoft and warm;
Thy pinky hand, and dimpled arm;

                              The

Thy filken locks that fcantly peep,

With gold-tip'd ends, where circle deep

Around thy neck in harmlefs grace

So foft and fleekly hold their place,

Might harder hearts with kindnefs fill,

　　And gain our right good will.

Each paffing clown beftows his bleffing,

Thy mouth is worn with old wives' kiffing:

E'en lighter looks the gloomy eye

Of furly fenfe, when thou art by;

And yet I think whoe'er they be,

　　They love thee not like me.

Perhaps when time fhall add a few

Short years to thee, thou'lt love me too.

Then wilt thou thro' life's weary way

Become my fure and cheering ftay:

Wilt care for me, and be my hold,

　　When I am weak and old.

Thou'lt

Thou'lt liften to my lengthen'd tale,

And pity me when I am frail——

But fee, the fweepy fpinning fly

Upon the window takes thine eye.

Go to thy little fenfelefs play——

    Thou doeft not heed my lay.

A CHILD

A CHILD TO HIS SICK GRAND-FATHER.

GRAND-DAD, they fay your old and frail,
Your ftocked legs begin to fail:
Your knobbed ftick (that was my horfe)
Can fcarce fupport your bended corfe;
While back to wall, you lean fo fad,
   I'm vex'd to fee you, dad.

You us'd to fmile, and ftroke my head,
And tell me how good children did;
But now I wot not how it be,
You take me feldom on your knee;

Yet

Yet ne'erthelefs I am right glad
  To fit befide you, dad.

How lank and thin your beard hangs down!
Scant are the white hairs on your crown:
How wan and hollow are your cheeks!
Your brow is rough with crofling breaks;
But yet, for all his ftrength is fled,
  I love my own old dad.

The houfewives round their potions brew,
And goffips come to afk for you:
And for your weal each neighbour cares,
And good men kneel, and fay their pray'rs:
And ev'ry body looks fo fad,
  When you are ailing, dad.

You will not die, and leave us then?
Roufe up and be our dad again.

                      When

When you are quiet and laid in bed,

We'll doff our ſhoes and ſoftly tread ;

And when you wake we'll aye be near,

   To fill old dad his cheer.

When thro' the houſe you ſhift your ſtand,

I'll lead you kindly by the hand :

When dinner's ſet, I'll with you bide,

And aye be ſerving by your ſide :

And when the weary fire burns blue,

   I'll ſit and talk with you.

I have a tale both long and good,

About a partlet and her brood ;

And cunning greedy fox, that ſtole,

By dead of midnight thro' a hole,

Which ſlyly to the hen-rooſt led—

   You love a ſtory, dad ?

                        And

And then I have a wond'rous tale

Of men all clad in coats of mail,

With glitt'ring fwords——you nod, I think?

Your fixed eyes begin to wink:

Down on your bofom finks your head:

You do not hear me, dad.

THE

THE HORSE AND HIS RIDER.

BRAC'D in the finewy vigour of thy breed,
In pride of gen'rous ftrength, thou ftately fteed,
Thy broad cheft to the battle's front is given,
Thy mane fair floating to the winds of heaven.
Thy champing hoofs the flinty pebbles break;
Graceful the rifing of thine arched neck.
White churning foam thy chaffed bits enlock;
And from thy noftril burfts the curling fmoke.
Thy kindling eye-balls brave the glaring fouth;
And dreadful is the thunder of thy mouth:
Whilft low to earth thy curving haunches bend,
Thy fweepy tail involv'd in clouds of fand;
Erect in air thou rear'ft thy front of pride,
And ring'ft the plated harnefs on thy fide.

But,

But, lo! what creature, goodly to the fight,

Dares thus beftride thee, chaffing in thy might?

Of portly ftature, and determin'd mien?

Whofe dark eye dwells beneath a brow ferene?

And forward looks unmov'd to fields of death:

And fmiling, gently ftrokes thee in thy wrath?

Whofe brandifh'd falch'on dreaded gleams afar?

It is a Britifh foldier, arm'd for war!

F I N I S.